RHYTHMS

for LIFE

PLANNER & JOURNAL

---

90 DAYS TO

PEACE AND PURPOSE

REBEKAH LYONS

NAME Jes Epting

EMAIL

PHONE 706.955.5695

YEAR 2024 QUARTER ○ 1 ○ 2 ○ 3 ○ 4

ZONDERVAN BOOKS

Rhythms for Life Planner and Journal

Requests for information should be addressed to:
Zondervan, *3900 Sparks Dr. SE, Grand Rapids, Michigan 49546*

Zondervan titles may be purchased in bulk for educational, business, fundraising, or sales promotional use. For information, please email SpecialMarkets@Zondervan.com.

ISBN 978-0-310-36116-9 (hardcover)

Author is represented by The Christopher Ferebee Agency, www.christopherferebee .com.

Cover design: Curt Diepenhorst
Cover illustration: Dana Tanamachi
Interior design: Aaron Campbell

Printed in Malaysia

20 21 22 23 24 25 26 27 28 /IMAGO/ 15 14 13 12 11 10 9 8 7 6 5 4 3

It's never too late to reestablish what you want your life to be about.

—REBEKAH LYONS

WELCOME

I'm thrilled to introduce the *Rhythms for Life Planner & Journal*. I trust this step of intention—a decision to practice your life in rhythm—will keep stress and anxiety at bay and lead to the peace and purpose you desire.

When we walk in rhythm, we come alive! When we're out of rhythm, our minds, bodies, relationships, and dreams pay the price. My book, *Rhythms of Renewal*, chronicles how I discovered four simple rhythms that radically changed my life and brought sustained emotional health.

REST. RESTORE. CONNECT. CREATE.

This planner is not a to-do list, but an un-do list! These pages invite you to release the things that drain you and rebuild the life you long for. The rhythm system offers a few moments each morning to reclaim your day before it claims you.

As you begin this daily practice, may you experience the renewal God offers! The fun part? You'll live these #rhythmsforlife in your own unique way, at a pace that works for you! This isn't a race, but a rhythm. Transformation happens one small step at a time.

LET'S BEGIN!

Rebekah

Be sure to utilize the free Rhythms for Life Planner & Journal *coaching video with Rebekah!*
Visit: www.RebekahLyons.com

CONTENTS

** Daily Routines, Journal Pages, and Weekend Reviews are interspersed in a weekly format beginning on page 30.*

RHYTHM SYSTEM

HOW TO USE THE RHYTHMS FOR LIFE JOURNAL AND PLANNER

Within this system, you'll create your own daily, weekly, monthly, and quarterly routines, using the quadrants of REST, RESTORE, CONNECT, AND CREATE. I've developed the Rhythm system, a 90-day strategy with daily practices you will grow to love! There are four components that make this process invaluable.

PREPARE

TAKE INVENTORY

You'll begin by reflecting on your current season by journaling through a series of prompts to help you assess: *What's Right? What's Wrong? What's Confused? What's Missing?* Your answers will become your guide to knowing how to focus your rhythm plans in the areas that will produce the most change. Then, each Sunday, you'll take inventory of the previous week as you plan with intention for the week ahead.

INPUT & OUTPUT RHYTHMS

REST slows us down, examines our hearts, allows us to get quiet, and inspires gratitude to receive spiritual health.
RESTORE offers foods for fuel, play, and adventure, and strengthens our bodies for physical health.
CONNECT forges friendships, vulnerability, forgiveness, and hospitality for sustained relational health.
CREATE helps us dream again, recover our purpose, and cultivate life-long learning for vocational health.
Rest and Restore are input rhythms that fill us up.
Connect and Create are output rhythms that serve others.

RHYTHMS LIST

These activities will provide inspiration as you consider your daily routine and monthly activities to Rest, Restore, Connect, and Create. Incorporate your own ideas into this list and return to pages 16–19 throughout your 90-day journey for both helpful and fun ideas to implement and enjoy.

PLAN

MORNING & EVENING ROUTINES

Establishing your ideal morning and evening routine is essential to your emotional health. The first hour of each morning sets the framework for your day. Establishing a routine for deep sleep each evening will determine the quality of your rest. Create your ideal routines for this quarter, then evaluate what's working on your daily pages, allowing adjustments for each particular day.

MONTHLY ACTIVITIES CALENDAR

Take a moment to plan ahead each month for creative expressions that will require more time and intention. Pick one monthly activity from each Rhythms list (or create your own) and schedule it on the calendar. Use these pages to incorporate your daily, weekly, and monthly plans, activities, appointments, and goals. Each Sunday you will be prompted to review and check in.

QUARTERLY PLANS

As you prepare for the next three months, consider a longer form activity that you would like to experience related to each rhythm. Be specific and note what you want to do, where, and with whom, then be prepared to add it in your monthly activities calendar to ensure it takes place.

DAILY ROUTINE

The daily pages allow you to claim your day. Each morning, you'll choose one rhythm activity from the suggestions or create your own and write it in the blank. Take a moment to write out your morning routine and plan your bedtime routine, given the circumstances of your day. If your mind is flooded with tasks, note your top three priorities for the day to keep them in view.

ENACT

JOURNAL PAGES

Your daily routine offers space to journal. A key component to the Rhythm system is quiet reflection. Take this space to pause, listen to God, reflect, and assess. Capture inspiration, ideas, prayers, or conversation with God, or simply use the space for the occasional list you may need to refer back to in the future.

WEEKEND REVIEW

We recommend taking Sunday to reflect on Monday through Saturday. Start by measuring your progress and determining what one rhythm needs intentional time before your weekend is complete. Next, answer the prompts to complete the review as a way of taking inventory before the week ahead. Sunday is also the perfect time for quiet reflection. We've provided two pages at the end of each week for longer form journaling before you head into the new week.

ASSESS

QUARTERLY REFLECTION

Well done! You've committed to prioritizing your mental health for three months. Are you feeling more rested, restored, connected, and creative? Less anxious, worried, and stressed?

Take time to listen, reflect, and assess. Identify and describe how well you did implementing the Rhythm system this past quarter, as well as how you plan to improve next quarter.

To order your *Rhythms for Life Planner & Journal* for a new quarter, visit:
WWW.REBEKAHLYONS.COM

TAKE INVENTORY

WHAT'S RIGHT?

Naming what's right keeps us grateful and grounded.

What is good? What are the gifts you've been given? What rhythm comes most naturally for you?

WHAT'S WRONG?

Naming what's wrong is the first step in solving a problem.

What challenges have you faced? In what areas have distractions kept you from living in rhythm?

WHAT'S CONFUSED?

Naming what's confused helps identify what needs clarity.

What thought or question do you continually return to? What is taking up mental energy? Where do you feel stuck in life?

WHAT'S MISSING?

Naming what's missing offers insight for what needs added.

Ask a trusted friend or spouse if they notice a blind spot. What do you love that you seldom have time to enjoy?

INPUT-OUTPUT RHYTHMS

Rest and Restore are input rhythms that fill us up.
Connect and Create are output rhythms that serve others.
Circle the rhythms that come most naturally for you in this season.
Underline the one(s) that need more intention:

INPUT	OUTPUT
REST	CONNECT
RESTORE	CREATE

Do you tend towards the input rhythms or the output? Why?

What's working well? What would you incorporate in the future?

EVALUATE YOUR RHYTHMS

See the Rhythms list in the following section for inspiration, then list ways when you can incorporate some of them in your life over the next three months.

	EXISTING RHYTHMS	NEW RHYTHMS
DAILY ROUTINES		
MONTHLY ACTIVITIES		
QUARTERLY PLANS		

INPUT RHYTHMS LIST

REST

DAILY

1. Take a walk
2. Reflect and journal
3. Light a candle
4. Take 10 long breaths
5. Play calming music
6. Get 8 hours of sleep
7. Confess your fears, then release them
8. Stay off social media until 10 a.m.
9. Meditate on Scripture
10. Unplug an hour before bed
11. Practice your morning routine
12. Practice your evening routine
13. Practice contemplative prayer
14. Watch the sunset
15. Read a book
16. Enjoy tea or coffee
17. Spend time alone
18. Get sunlight
19. Declutter my desk
20. List today's triumphs

WEEKLY

1. Practice Sabbath
2. Take a nap
3. Spend time in nature
4. Read a novel
5. Take a bath
6. Watch a movie

MONTHLY

1. Make a gratitude list
2. Take inventory of your life
3. Get a massage
4. Add plants to your indoors
5. Enjoy a picnic
6. Take in a scenic view

OTHERS

INPUT RHYTHMS LIST

RESTORE

DAILY

1. Walk 10,000 steps
2. Cut sugar for the day
3. Drink 4 glasses of water
4. Watch a comedy
5. Take a walk around the block
6. Grab an afternoon snack
7. Touch your toes (stretch)
8. Do a word search
9. Cook a favorite meal
10. Go swimming
11. Make your own salad
12. Have a dance party
13. Stock a bowl with fruit in your kitchen
14. Try a new experience
15. Play an inspiring song
16. Skip watching the news
17. Listen to classical music
18. Try a new recipe
19. Break a sweat
20. Laugh

WEEKLY

1. Create a healthy meal plan
2. Play a board game
3. Take a hike in nature
4. Attend a fair or farmer's market
5. Go on a bike ride
6. Do a 40-minute workout

MONTHLY

1. Take a day trip to a nearby town
2. Take a vacation
3. Visit an apple orchard
4. Go sledding or skiing
5. Spend time by water
6. Plan a weekend adventure

OTHERS

OUTPUT RHYTHMS LIST

CONNECT

DAILY

1. Text and encourage a friend
2. Smile at a stranger
3. Give a compliment
4. Journal a memory
5. Read a book to your kids
6. Implement a "no phones at the table" policy
7. Take a walk with someone
8. Dance with your spouse
9. Have tea or coffee with someone
10. FaceTime or call a relative
11. Apologize and forgive
12. Mend a relationship that needs it
13. Initiate a meaningful conversation
14. Go to the gym with a friend
15. Pray with someone in pain
16. Write a note to a loved one
17. Add value to someone
18. Make someone laugh
19. Listen intently to a loved one
20. Send a silly card

WEEKLY

1. Have lunch with a friend
2. Go on a date night
3. Have a family movie night
4. Build a fire and make s'mores
5. Send flowers to someone
6. Invite friends to watch a game

MONTHLY

1. Plan a girls' or guys' night out
2. Volunteer at your local church
3. Serve at a shelter or food pantry
4. Attend a marriage retreat
5. Host a meal at your home
6. Babysit for a friend

OTHERS

OUTPUT RHYTHMS LIST

CREATE

DAILY

1. Use your imagination
2. Let your mind wander and daydream
3. Color with a child
4. Take photographs
5. Journal your goals
6. Write what you dreamed last night
7. Knit, crochet, or sew
8. Play pretend with a child in your life
9. Clean out a drawer, closet, or room
10. Learn something new
11. Take a class
12. Write a story, poem, or song
13. Make your favorite drink at home
14. Style a bookshelf
15. Bake something
16. Look for inspiration
17. Keep an idea notebook
18. Collect found items
19. Doodle or draw
20. Read something new

WEEKLY

1. Create a memory wall with pics
2. Paint something
3. Create a favorite playlist
4. Build with your hands
5. Build a snowman
6. Donate items you no longer need

MONTHLY

1. Plant a garden or flower bed
2. Decorate a room in your home
3. Create a photo book of a memory
4. Start a new holiday tradition
5. Create a family recipe book
6. Try a new hobby

OTHERS

MORNING ROUTINE

How you begin your day is essential to your emotional health. By establishing your ideal morning routine, you will have a go-to guide to help you kick off your day. How you spend your first 60 minutes will shape the coming 15 hours, so be intentional and realistic.

What rhythms do you want to practice in the early morning?

WEEKDAY RHYTHMS

1.
2.
3.
4.
5.

WEEKEND RHYTHMS

1.
2.
3.
4.
5.

WEEKDAY SCHEDULE

___AM

___AM

___AM

WEEKEND RHYTHMS

___AM

___AM

___AM

EVENING ROUTINE

Rest is your superpower. Establish your ideal evening routine below as a guide for a relaxed evening before you go to sleep. Consider what time you want to eat your final meal, turn off digital devices, pray, connect with a loved one, or read a good book.

What rhythms and habits do you want to practice in the evening?

WEEKDAY RHYTHMS

1.
2.
3.
4.
5.

WEEKEND RHYTHMS

1.
2.
3.
4.
5.

WEEKDAY SCHEDULE

___ PM

___ PM

___ PM

WEEKEND RHYTHMS

___ PM

___ PM

___ PM

MONTHLY ACTIVITIES

MONTH

MONDAY	TUESDAY	WEDNESDAY	THURSDAY

The unexamined life is not worth living.

—SOCRATES

FRIDAY	SATURDAY	SUNDAY

MONTHLY RHYTHM GOALS

Implement one of each rhythm that requires more intention. Refer to the Rhythms list, monthly section, on pages 16–19.

REST

RESTORE

CONNECT

CREATE

MONTHLY ACTIVITIES

MONTH

MONDAY	TUESDAY	WEDNESDAY	THURSDAY

We were created for connection, and when we are closely knit within our community, we are at our best, flourishing and full of life.

—REBEKAH LYONS

FRIDAY	SATURDAY	SUNDAY

MONTHLY RHYTHM GOALS

Implement one of each rhythm that requires more intention. Refer to the Rhythms list, monthly section, on pages 16–19.

REST

RESTORE

CONNECT

CREATE

MONTHLY ACTIVITIES

MONTH

MONDAY	TUESDAY	WEDNESDAY	THURSDAY

Rest time is not waste time. It is economy to gather fresh strength . . . It is wisdom to take occasional furlough. In the long run, we shall do more by sometimes doing less.

—CHARLES SPURGEON

FRIDAY	SATURDAY	SUNDAY

MONTHLY RHYTHM GOALS

Implement one of each rhythm that requires more intention. Refer to the Rhythms list, monthly section, on pages 16–19.

REST

RESTORE

CONNECT

CREATE

QUARTERLY PLANS

Over the next three months, consider the big moments. Will you . . . Take a trip? Host a holiday or gathering? Go on an adventure? Sign up for a class? Begin a creative project? Implement a tech detox?

REST

Give yourself a day off from any responsibility and take inventory of your current well-being.

What:

Where:

With Whom:

RESTORE

Plan an adventure, day trip, or getaway. Ensure you have plans to break a sweat.

What:

Where:

With Whom:

Planning ahead will help ensure that you are creating clear goals as well as a strategy. In this section, allow yourself ample time to think through your intentions and create a plan for implementing Rhythms for Life during the next quarter.

CONNECT

Plan a fun activity or gathering with a friend or group that ensures ample time for meaningful conversation.

What:

Where:

With Whom:

CREATE

Take on a project that involves working with your hands. Use my imagination to make something out of nothing.

What:

Where:

With Whom:

Be sure these plans are incorporated into your 90-day calendar.

MONDAY

DATE

When you're vulnerable and alone, you're afraid.
When you're vulnerable and together, you're brave.

—REBEKAH LYONS

REST

Today I will . . .

- ○ Meditate on Scripture
- ○ Reflect and journal
- ○ Read a book
- ○ Stretch my muscles

RESTORE

Today I will . . .

- ○ Stock a fruit bowl
- ○ Take a walk
- ○ Drink 4 glasses of water
- ○ Break a sweat

CONNECT

Today I will . . .

- ○ Write a friend a note
- ○ Encourage someone
- ○ Apologize and forgive
- ○ Pray with someone

CREATE

Today I will . . .

- ○ Journal my goals
- ○ Read something new
- ○ Organize a space
- ○ Daydream

MORNING ROUTINE

BEDTIME ROUTINE

PRIORITIES

QUIET REFLECTION

PAUSE · EXAMINE · JOURNAL

TUESDAY

DATE

Without great solitude, no serious work is possible.

—PABLO PICASSO

REST

Today I will . . .

- ○ Enjoy tea or coffee
- ○ Reflect and journal
- ○ Get sunlight
- ○ List today's triumphs

RESTORE

Today I will . . .

- ○ Play an inspiring song
- ○ Take a walk
- ○ Make a salad
- ○ Have a dance party

CONNECT

Today I will . . .

- ○ Work out with a friend
- ○ Encourage someone
- ○ FaceTime a friend
- ○ Make someone laugh

CREATE

Today I will . . .

- ○ Take a class
- ○ Read something new
- ○ Color with a child
- ○ Write down ideas

MORNING ROUTINE

BEDTIME ROUTINE

PRIORITIES

QUIET REFLECTION

PAUSE · EXAMINE · JOURNAL

WEDNESDAY

DATE

When anxiety was great within me,
your consolation brought me joy.

—PSALM 94:19

REST

Today I will . . .

- ○ Spend time alone
- ○ Reflect and journal
- ○ Declutter my desk
- ○ Get 8 hours of sleep

RESTORE

Today I will . . .

- ○ Stretch
- ○ Take a walk
- ○ Cook a favorite meal
- ○ Laugh

CONNECT

Today I will . . .

- ○ Give a compliment
- ○ Encourage someone
- ○ Listen intently
- ○ Have coffee with a friend

CREATE

Today I will . . .

- ○ Use my imagination
- ○ Read something new
- ○ Doodle or draw
- ○ Bake something

MORNING ROUTINE

BEDTIME ROUTINE

PRIORITIES

QUIET REFLECTION

PAUSE · EXAMINE · JOURNAL

THURSDAY

DATE

Finish each day and be done with it. You have done what you could. Some blunders and absurdities no doubt crept in; forget them as soon as you can.

—RALPH WALDO EMERSON

REST

Today I will . . .

- ○ Practice contemplative prayer
- ○ Reflect and journal
- ○ Play calming music
- ○ Limit phone use after dinner

RESTORE

Today I will . . .

- ○ Cut sugar for the day
- ○ Take a walk
- ○ Do a word search
- ○ Watch a comedy

CONNECT

Today I will . . .

- ○ Enjoy deep conversation
- ○ Encourage someone
- ○ Smile at a stranger
- ○ Dance with someone

CREATE

Today I will . . .

- ○ Write down my dreams
- ○ Read something new
- ○ Play pretend with a child
- ○ Look for inspiration

MORNING ROUTINE

BEDTIME ROUTINE

PRIORITIES

QUIET REFLECTION

PAUSE · EXAMINE · JOURNAL

FRIDAY

DATE

It is exercise alone that supports the spirits, and keeps the mind in vigor.

—MARCUS TULLIUS CICERO

REST

Today I will . . .

- ○ Confess my fears
- ○ Reflect and journal
- ○ Limit tech use before work
- ○ Take 10 long breaths

RESTORE

Today I will . . .

- ○ Skip watching the news
- ○ Take a walk
- ○ Try a new experience
- ○ Grab an afternoon snack

CONNECT

Today I will . . .

- ○ Have lunch with a friend
- ○ Encourage someone
- ○ Read to a child
- ○ Limit phones at the table

CREATE

Today I will . . .

- ○ Take photographs
- ○ Read something new
- ○ Make a favorite drink
- ○ Learn something new

MORNING ROUTINE

BEDTIME ROUTINE

PRIORITIES

QUIET REFLECTION

PAUSE · EXAMINE · JOURNAL

SATURDAY

DATE

The primary impulse of hospitality is to create a safe and welcoming place where a stranger can be converted into a friend.

—JOSHUA W. JIPP

REST

Today I will . . .

- ○ Light a candle
- ○ Reflect and journal
- ○ Take a nap
- ○ Watch the sunset

RESTORE

Today I will . . .

- ○ Create a meal plan
- ○ Take a walk
- ○ Try a new recipe
- ○ Play a board game

CONNECT

Today I will . . .

- ○ Journal a memory
- ○ Encourage someone
- ○ Walk with someone
- ○ Have a family movie night

CREATE

Today I will . . .

- ○ Build with my hands
- ○ Read something new
- ○ Style a bookshelf
- ○ Create a playlist

MORNING ROUTINE

BEDTIME ROUTINE

PRIORITIES

QUIET REFLECTION

PAUSE · EXAMINE · JOURNAL

SUNDAY

WEEK ONE

HOW WELL DID YOU DO THIS WEEK?

Check the boxes to indicate which rhythms you completed each day. The tallied total will give you a comprehensive view of your week!

	M	T	W	TH	F	S	TOTAL
REST	☐	☐	☐	☐	☐	☐	/6
RESTORE	☐	☐	☐	☐	☐	☐	/6
CONNECT	☐	☐	☐	☐	☐	☐	/6
CREATE	☐	☐	☐	☐	☐	☐	/6

REPLENISH YOUR WEAKEST RHYTHM

Which of the above rhythms did you practice the least and how can you incorporate that rhythm today to be replenished for the week ahead?

WEEKEND REVIEW

REFLECT · ASSESS · LEARN

What did you learn about yourself this week? How were your relationships impacted by your practice of each rhythm?

Which rhythm and activity felt most natural for you? How can this become a part of your routine going forward?

How well did you practice your morning and bedtime routines? What adjustments can you make to ensure you practice these daily?

Check your monthly calendar for upcoming activities and goals.

WEEKEND JOURNAL

DATE

There is no fear in love.
But perfect love drives out fear.

—1 JOHN 4:18

MONDAY

DATE

Never forget the nine most important words of any family—
I love you. You are beautiful. Please forgive me.

—H. JACKSON BROWN, JR.

REST

Today I will . . .

- ○ Meditate on Scripture
- ○ Reflect and journal
- ○ Read a book
- ○ Stretch my muscles

RESTORE

Today I will . . .

- ○ Stock a fruit bowl
- ○ Take a walk
- ○ Drink 4 glasses of water
- ○ Break a sweat

CONNECT

Today I will . . .

- ○ Write a friend a note
- ○ Encourage someone
- ○ Apologize and forgive
- ○ Pray with someone

CREATE

Today I will . . .

- ○ Journal my goals
- ○ Read something new
- ○ Organize a space
- ○ Daydream

MORNING ROUTINE

BEDTIME ROUTINE

PRIORITIES

QUIET REFLECTION

PAUSE · EXAMINE · JOURNAL

TUESDAY

DATE

For God has not given us a spirit of fear,
but of power and of love and of a sound mind.

—2 TIMOTHY 1:7 NKJV

REST

Today I will . . .

- ○ Enjoy tea or coffee
- ○ Reflect and journal
- ○ Get sunlight
- ○ List today's triumphs

RESTORE

Today I will . . .

- ○ Play an inspiring song
- ○ Take a walk
- ○ Make a salad
- ○ Have a dance party

CONNECT

Today I will . . .

- ○ Work out with a friend
- ○ Encourage someone
- ○ FaceTime a friend
- ○ Make someone laugh

CREATE

Today I will . . .

- ○ Take a class
- ○ Read something new
- ○ Color with a child
- ○ Write down ideas

MORNING ROUTINE

BEDTIME ROUTINE

PRIORITIES

QUIET REFLECTION

PAUSE · EXAMINE · JOURNAL

WEDNESDAY

DATE

God cares more about our presence than our performance.

—REBEKAH LYONS

REST

Today I will . . .

- ○ Spend time alone
- ○ Reflect and journal
- ○ Declutter my desk
- ○ Get 8 hours of sleep

RESTORE

Today I will . . .

- ○ Stretch
- ○ Take a walk
- ○ Cook a favorite meal
- ○ Laugh

CONNECT

Today I will . . .

- ○ Give a compliment
- ○ Encourage someone
- ○ Listen intently
- ○ Have coffee with a friend

CREATE

Today I will . . .

- ○ Use my imagination
- ○ Read something new
- ○ Doodle or draw
- ○ Bake something

MORNING ROUTINE

BEDTIME ROUTINE

PRIORITIES

QUIET REFLECTION

PAUSE · EXAMINE · JOURNAL

THURSDAY

DATE

We are created to live rhythmically, with intention.

—CURT THOMPSON, MD

REST

Today I will . . .

- ○ Practice contemplative prayer
- ○ Reflect and journal
- ○ Play calming music
- ○ No tech before bed

RESTORE

Today I will . . .

- ○ Cut sugar for the day
- ○ Take a walk
- ○ Do a word search
- ○ Watch a comedy

CONNECT

Today I will . . .

- ○ Enjoy deep conversation
- ○ Encourage someone
- ○ Smile at a stranger
- ○ Dance with someone

CREATE

Today I will . . .

- ○ Write down my dreams
- ○ Read something new
- ○ Play pretend with a child
- ○ Look for inspiration

MORNING ROUTINE

BEDTIME ROUTINE

PRIORITIES

QUIET REFLECTION

PAUSE · EXAMINE · JOURNAL

FRIDAY

DATE

Perfect friendship is the friendship of those who are alike in virtue.

—ARISTOTLE

REST

Today I will . . .

- ○ Confess your fears
- ○ Reflect and journal
- ○ No tech morning
- ○ Take 10 long breaths

RESTORE

Today I will . . .

- ○ Skip watching the news
- ○ Take a walk
- ○ Try a new experience
- ○ Grab an afternoon snack

CONNECT

Today I will . . .

- ○ Have lunch with a friend
- ○ Encourage someone
- ○ Read to a child
- ○ No phones at the table

CREATE

Today I will . . .

- ○ Take photographs
- ○ Read something new
- ○ Make a favorite drink
- ○ Learn something new

MORNING ROUTINE

BEDTIME ROUTINE

PRIORITIES

QUIET REFLECTION

PAUSE · EXAMINE · JOURNAL

SATURDAY

DATE

A world without a Sabbath would be like a man without a smile, like a summer without flowers, and like a homestead without a garden. It is the most joyous day of the week.

—HENRY WARD BEECHER

REST

Today I will . . .

- ○ Light a candle
- ○ Reflect and journal
- ○ Take a nap
- ○ Watch the sunset

RESTORE

Today I will . . .

- ○ Create a meal plan
- ○ Take a walk
- ○ Try a new recipe
- ○ Play a board game

CONNECT

Today I will . . .

- ○ Journal a memory
- ○ Encourage someone
- ○ Walk with someone
- ○ Have a family movie night

CREATE

Today I will . . .

- ○ Build with my hands
- ○ Read something new
- ○ Style a bookshelf
- ○ Create a playlist

MORNING ROUTINE

BEDTIME ROUTINE

PRIORITIES

QUIET REFLECTION

PAUSE · EXAMINE · JOURNAL

SUNDAY

WEEK TWO

HOW WELL DID YOU DO THIS WEEK?

Check the boxes to indicate which rhythms you completed each day. The tallied total will give you a comprehensive view of your week!

	M	T	W	TH	F	S	TOTAL
REST	☐	☐	☐	☐	☐	☐	/6
RESTORE	☐	☐	☐	☐	☐	☐	/6
CONNECT	☐	☐	☐	☐	☐	☐	/6
CREATE	☐	☐	☐	☐	☐	☐	/6

REPLENISH YOUR WEAKEST RHYTHM

Which of the above rhythms did you practice the least and how can you incorporate that rhythm today to be replenished for the week ahead?

WEEKEND REVIEW

REFLECT · ASSESS · LEARN

What did you learn about yourself this week? How were your relationships impacted by your practice of each rhythm?

Which rhythm and activity felt most natural for you? How can this become a part of your routine going forward?

How well did you practice your morning and bedtime routines? What adjustments can you make to ensure you practice these daily?

Check your monthly calendar for upcoming activities and goals.

WEEKEND JOURNAL

DATE

Do not be anxious about anything, but in every situation, by prayer and petition, with thanksgiving, present your requests to God. And the peace of God, which transcends all understanding, will guard your hearts and your minds in Christ Jesus.

—PHILIPPIANS 4:6–7

MONDAY

DATE

Life is never made unbearable by circumstances, but only by lack of meaning and purpose.

—VIKTOR FRANKL

REST

Today I will . . .

- ○ Meditate on Scripture
- ○ Reflect and journal
- ○ Read a book
- ○ Stretch my muscles

RESTORE

Today I will . . .

- ○ Stock a fruit bowl
- ○ Take a walk
- ○ Drink 4 glasses of water
- ○ Break a sweat

CONNECT

Today I will . . .

- ○ Write a friend a note
- ○ Encourage someone
- ○ Apologize and forgive
- ○ Pray with someone

CREATE

Today I will . . .

- ○ Journal my goals
- ○ Read something new
- ○ Organize a space
- ○ Daydream

MORNING ROUTINE

BEDTIME ROUTINE

PRIORITIES

QUIET REFLECTION

PAUSE · EXAMINE · JOURNAL

TUESDAY

DATE

We don't need to hustle to prove something God already says is true.

—REBEKAH LYONS

REST

Today I will . . .

- ○ Enjoy tea or coffee
- ○ Reflect and journal
- ○ Get sunlight
- ○ List today's triumphs

RESTORE

Today I will . . .

- ○ Play an inspiring song
- ○ Take a walk
- ○ Make a salad
- ○ Have a dance party

CONNECT

Today I will . . .

- ○ Work out with a friend
- ○ Encourage someone
- ○ FaceTime a friend
- ○ Make someone laugh

CREATE

Today I will . . .

- ○ Take a class
- ○ Read something new
- ○ Color with a child
- ○ Write down ideas

MORNING ROUTINE

BEDTIME ROUTINE

PRIORITIES

QUIET REFLECTION

PAUSE · EXAMINE · JOURNAL

WEDNESDAY

DATE

It is never too late to be what you might have been.

—GEORGE ELIOT

REST

Today I will . . .

- ○ Spend time alone
- ○ Reflect and journal
- ○ Declutter my desk
- ○ Get 8 hours of sleep

RESTORE

Today I will . . .

- ○ Stretch
- ○ Take a walk
- ○ Cook a favorite meal
- ○ Laugh

CONNECT

Today I will . . .

- ○ Give a compliment
- ○ Encourage someone
- ○ Listen intently
- ○ Have coffee with a friend

CREATE

Today I will . . .

- ○ Use my imagination
- ○ Read something new
- ○ Doodle or draw
- ○ Bake something

MORNING ROUTINE

BEDTIME ROUTINE

PRIORITIES

QUIET REFLECTION

PAUSE · EXAMINE · JOURNAL

THURSDAY

DATE

We are continually being nudged by our devices toward a set of choices. The question is whether those choices are leading us to the life we actually want.

—ANDY CROUCH

REST

Today I will . . .

- ○ Practice contemplative prayer
- ○ Reflect and journal
- ○ Play calming music
- ○ No tech before bed

RESTORE

Today I will . . .

- ○ Cut sugar for the day
- ○ Take a walk
- ○ Do a word search
- ○ Watch a comedy

CONNECT

Today I will . . .

- ○ Enjoy deep conversation
- ○ Encourage someone
- ○ Smile at a stranger
- ○ Dance with someone

CREATE

Today I will . . .

- ○ Write down my dreams
- ○ Read something new
- ○ Play pretend with a child
- ○ Look for inspiration

MORNING ROUTINE

BEDTIME ROUTINE

PRIORITIES

QUIET REFLECTION

PAUSE · EXAMINE · JOURNAL

FRIDAY

DATE

An anxious heart weighs a man down,
but a kind word cheers him up.

—PROVERBS 12:25

REST

Today I will . . .

- ○ Confess my fears
- ○ Reflect and journal
- ○ No tech morning
- ○ Take 10 long breaths

RESTORE

Today I will . . .

- ○ Skip watching the news
- ○ Take a walk
- ○ Try a new experience
- ○ Grab an afternoon snack

CONNECT

Today I will . . .

- ○ Have lunch with a friend
- ○ Encourage someone
- ○ Read to a child
- ○ No phones at the table

CREATE

Today I will . . .

- ○ Take photographs
- ○ Read something new
- ○ Make a favorite drink
- ○ Learn something new

MORNING ROUTINE

BEDTIME ROUTINE

PRIORITIES

QUIET REFLECTION

PAUSE · EXAMINE · JOURNAL

SATURDAY

DATE

Every now and then go away and have a little relaxation. To remain constantly at work will diminish your judgment.

—LEONARDO DA VINCI

REST

Today I will . . .

- ○ Light a candle
- ○ Reflect and journal
- ○ Take a nap
- ○ Watch the sunset

RESTORE

Today I will . . .

- ○ Create a meal plan
- ○ Take a walk
- ○ Try a new recipe
- ○ Play a board game

CONNECT

Today I will . . .

- ○ Journal a memory
- ○ Encourage someone
- ○ Walk with someone
- ○ Have a family movie night

CREATE

Today I will . . .

- ○ Build with my hands
- ○ Read something new
- ○ Style a bookshelf
- ○ Create a playlist

MORNING ROUTINE

BEDTIME ROUTINE

PRIORITIES

QUIET REFLECTION

PAUSE · EXAMINE · JOURNAL

SUNDAY

WEEK THREE

HOW WELL DID YOU DO THIS WEEK?

Check the boxes to indicate which rhythms you completed each day. The tallied total will give you a comprehensive view of your week!

	M	T	W	TH	F	S	TOTAL
REST	☐	☐	☐	☐	☐	☐	/6
RESTORE	☐	☐	☐	☐	☐	☐	/6
CONNECT	☐	☐	☐	☐	☐	☐	/6
CREATE	☐	☐	☐	☐	☐	☐	/6

REPLENISH YOUR WEAKEST RHYTHM

Which of the above rhythms did you practice the least and how can you incorporate that rhythm today to be replenished for the week ahead?

WEEKEND REVIEW

REFLECT · ASSESS · LEARN

What did you learn about yourself this week? How were your relationships impacted by your practice of each rhythm?

Which rhythm and activity felt most natural for you? How can this become a part of your routine going forward?

How well did you practice your morning and bedtime routines? What adjustments can you make to ensure you practice these daily?

Check your monthly calendar for upcoming activities and goals.

WEEKEND JOURNAL

DATE

The Lord your God is in your midst, A victorious warrior.
He will exult over you with joy; He will be quiet in
His love, He will rejoice over you with shouts of joy.

—ZEPHANIAH 3:17 NASB

MONDAY

DATE

Don't ask what the world needs. Ask what makes you come alive, and go do it. Because what the world needs is people who have come alive.

—HOWARD THURMAN

REST

Today I will . . .

- ○ Meditate on Scripture
- ○ Reflect and journal
- ○ Read a book
- ○ Stretch my muscles

RESTORE

Today I will . . .

- ○ Stock a fruit bowl
- ○ Take a walk
- ○ Drink 4 glasses of water
- ○ Break a sweat

CONNECT

Today I will . . .

- ○ Write a friend a note
- ○ Encourage someone
- ○ Apologize and forgive
- ○ Pray with someone

CREATE

Today I will . . .

- ○ Journal my goals
- ○ Read something new
- ○ Organize a space
- ○ Daydream

MORNING ROUTINE

BEDTIME ROUTINE

PRIORITIES

QUIET REFLECTION

PAUSE · EXAMINE · JOURNAL

TUESDAY

DATE

One cannot think well, love well, sleep well, if one has not dined well.

—VIRGINIA WOOLF

REST

Today I will . . .

- ○ Enjoy tea or coffee
- ○ Reflect and journal
- ○ Get sunlight
- ○ List today's triumphs

RESTORE

Today I will . . .

- ○ Play an inspiring song
- ○ Take a walk
- ○ Make a salad
- ○ Have a dance party

CONNECT

Today I will . . .

- ○ Work out with a friend
- ○ Encourage someone
- ○ FaceTime a friend
- ○ Make someone laugh

CREATE

Today I will . . .

- ○ Take a class
- ○ Read something new
- ○ Color with a child
- ○ Write down ideas

MORNING ROUTINE

BEDTIME ROUTINE

PRIORITIES

QUIET REFLECTION

PAUSE · EXAMINE · JOURNAL

WEDNESDAY

DATE

Bravery is moving scared.

—REBEKAH LYONS

REST

Today I will . . .

- ○ Spend time alone
- ○ Reflect and journal
- ○ Declutter my desk
- ○ Get 8 hours of sleep

RESTORE

Today I will . . .

- ○ Stretch
- ○ Take a walk
- ○ Cook a favorite meal
- ○ Laugh

CONNECT

Today I will . . .

- ○ Give a compliment
- ○ Encourage someone
- ○ Listen intently
- ○ Have coffee with a friend

CREATE

Today I will . . .

- ○ Use my imagination
- ○ Read something new
- ○ Doodle or draw
- ○ Bake something

MORNING ROUTINE

BEDTIME ROUTINE

PRIORITIES

QUIET REFLECTION

PAUSE · EXAMINE · JOURNAL

THURSDAY

DATE

His love motivates her respect; her respect motivates his love.

—EMERSON EGGERICHS

REST

Today I will . . .

- ○ Practice contemplative prayer
- ○ Reflect and journal
- ○ Play calming music
- ○ No tech before bed

RESTORE

Today I will . . .

- ○ Cut sugar for the day
- ○ Take a walk
- ○ Do a word search
- ○ Watch a comedy

CONNECT

Today I will . . .

- ○ Enjoy deep conversation
- ○ Encourage someone
- ○ Smile at a stranger
- ○ Dance with someone

CREATE

Today I will . . .

- ○ Write down my dreams
- ○ Read something new
- ○ Play pretend with a child
- ○ Look for inspiration

MORNING ROUTINE

BEDTIME ROUTINE

PRIORITIES

QUIET REFLECTION

PAUSE · EXAMINE · JOURNAL

FRIDAY

DATE

When I am afraid, I put my trust in you.

—PSALM 56:3

REST

Today I will . . .

- ○ Confess my fears
- ○ Reflect and journal
- ○ No tech morning
- ○ Take 10 long breaths

RESTORE

Today I will . . .

- ○ Skip watching the news
- ○ Take a walk
- ○ Try a new experience
- ○ Grab an afternoon snack

CONNECT

Today I will . . .

- ○ Have lunch with a friend
- ○ Encourage someone
- ○ Read to a child
- ○ No phones at the table

CREATE

Today I will . . .

- ○ Take photographs
- ○ Read something new
- ○ Make a favorite drink
- ○ Learn something new

MORNING ROUTINE

BEDTIME ROUTINE

PRIORITIES

QUIET REFLECTION

PAUSE · EXAMINE · JOURNAL

SATURDAY

DATE

It is a happy talent to know how to play.

—RALPH WALDO EMERSON

REST

Today I will . . .

- ○ Light a candle
- ○ Reflect and journal
- ○ Take a nap
- ○ Watch the sunset

RESTORE

Today I will . . .

- ○ Create a meal plan
- ○ Take a walk
- ○ Try a new recipe
- ○ Play a board game

CONNECT

Today I will . . .

- ○ Journal a memory
- ○ Encourage someone
- ○ Walk with someone
- ○ Have a family movie night

CREATE

Today I will . . .

- ○ Build with my hands
- ○ Read something new
- ○ Style a bookshelf
- ○ Create a playlist

MORNING ROUTINE

BEDTIME ROUTINE

PRIORITIES

QUIET REFLECTION

PAUSE · EXAMINE · JOURNAL

SUNDAY

WEEK FOUR

HOW WELL DID YOU DO THIS WEEK?

Check the boxes to indicate which rhythms you completed each day. The tallied total will give you a comprehensive view of your week!

	M	T	W	TH	F	S	TOTAL
REST	☐	☐	☐	☐	☐	☐	/6
RESTORE	☐	☐	☐	☐	☐	☐	/6
CONNECT	☐	☐	☐	☐	☐	☐	/6
CREATE	☐	☐	☐	☐	☐	☐	/6

REPLENISH YOUR WEAKEST RHYTHM

Which of the above rhythms did you practice the least and how can you incorporate that rhythm today to be replenished for the week ahead?

WEEKEND REVIEW

REFLECT · ASSESS · LEARN

What did you learn about yourself this week? How were your relationships impacted by your practice of each rhythm?

Which rhythm and activity felt most natural for you? How can this become a part of your routine going forward?

How well did you practice your morning and bedtime routines? What adjustments can you make to ensure you practice these daily?

Check your monthly calendar for upcoming activities and goals.

WEEKEND JOURNAL

DATE

Have I not commanded you? Be strong and courageous. Do not be terrified; do not be discouraged, for the Lord your God will be with you wherever you go.

—JOSHUA 1:9

MONDAY

DATE

So do not fear, for I am with you; do not be dismayed, for I am your God. I will strengthen you and help you; I will uphold you with my righteous right hand.

—ISAIAH 41:10

REST

Today I will . . .

- ○ Meditate on Scripture
- ○ Reflect and journal
- ○ Read a book
- ○ Stretch my muscles

RESTORE

Today I will . . .

- ○ Stock a fruit bowl
- ○ Take a walk
- ○ Drink 4 glasses of water
- ○ Break a sweat

CONNECT

Today I will . . .

- ○ Write a friend a note
- ○ Encourage someone
- ○ Apologize and forgive
- ○ Pray with someone

CREATE

Today I will . . .

- ○ Journal my goals
- ○ Read something new
- ○ Organize a space
- ○ Daydream

MORNING ROUTINE

BEDTIME ROUTINE

PRIORITIES

QUIET REFLECTION

PAUSE · EXAMINE · JOURNAL

TUESDAY

DATE

Tell the truth and write about freedom and fight for it, however you can, and you will be richly rewarded.

—ANNE LAMOTT

REST

Today I will . . .

- ○ Enjoy tea or coffee
- ○ Reflect and journal
- ○ Get sunlight
- ○ List today's triumphs

RESTORE

Today I will . . .

- ○ Play an inspiring song
- ○ Take a walk
- ○ Make a salad
- ○ Have a dance party

CONNECT

Today I will . . .

- ○ Work out with a friend
- ○ Encourage someone
- ○ FaceTime a friend
- ○ Make someone laugh

CREATE

Today I will . . .

- ○ Take a class
- ○ Read something new
- ○ Color with a child
- ○ Write down ideas

MORNING ROUTINE

BEDTIME ROUTINE

PRIORITIES

QUIET REFLECTION

PAUSE · EXAMINE · JOURNAL

WEDNESDAY

DATE

God asks what it is He's made us to love . . . And then . . . He whispers, "Let's go do that together."

—BOB GOFF

REST

Today I will . . .

- ○ Spend time alone
- ○ Reflect and journal
- ○ Declutter my desk
- ○ Get 8 hours of sleep

RESTORE

Today I will . . .

- ○ Stretch
- ○ Take a walk
- ○ Cook a favorite meal
- ○ Laugh

CONNECT

Today I will . . .

- ○ Give a compliment
- ○ Encourage someone
- ○ Listen intently
- ○ Have coffee with a friend

CREATE

Today I will . . .

- ○ Use my imagination
- ○ Read something new
- ○ Doodle or draw
- ○ Bake something

MORNING ROUTINE

BEDTIME ROUTINE

PRIORITIES

QUIET REFLECTION

PAUSE · EXAMINE · JOURNAL

THURSDAY

DATE

I do not understand why others are able to find new life in the midst of a living death, though I am one of them.

—PARKER PALMER

REST

Today I will . . .

- ○ Practice contemplative prayer
- ○ Reflect and journal
- ○ Play calming music
- ○ No tech before bed

RESTORE

Today I will . . .

- ○ Cut sugar for the day
- ○ Take a walk
- ○ Do a word search
- ○ Watch a comedy

CONNECT

Today I will . . .

- ○ Enjoy deep conversation
- ○ Encourage someone
- ○ Smile at a stranger
- ○ Dance with someone

CREATE

Today I will . . .

- ○ Write down my dreams
- ○ Read something new
- ○ Play pretend with a child
- ○ Look for inspiration

MORNING ROUTINE

BEDTIME ROUTINE

PRIORITIES

QUIET REFLECTION

PAUSE · EXAMINE · JOURNAL

FRIDAY

DATE

It doesn't matter what the outside reveals if the inside is starved of strength.

—REBEKAH LYONS

REST

Today I will . . .

- ○ Confess my fears
- ○ Reflect and journal
- ○ No tech morning
- ○ Take 10 long breaths

RESTORE

Today I will . . .

- ○ Skip watching the news
- ○ Take a walk
- ○ Try a new experience
- ○ Grab an afternoon snack

CONNECT

Today I will . . .

- ○ Have lunch with a friend
- ○ Encourage someone
- ○ Read to a child
- ○ No phones at the table

CREATE

Today I will . . .

- ○ Take photographs
- ○ Read something new
- ○ Make a favorite drink
- ○ Learn something new

MORNING ROUTINE

BEDTIME ROUTINE

PRIORITIES

QUIET REFLECTION

PAUSE · EXAMINE · JOURNAL

SATURDAY

DATE

Live a quiet life and work with your hands.

—DANA TANAMACHI

REST

Today I will . . .

- ○ Light a candle
- ○ Reflect and journal
- ○ Take a nap
- ○ Watch the sunset

RESTORE

Today I will . . .

- ○ Create a meal plan
- ○ Take a walk
- ○ Try a new recipe
- ○ Play a board game

CONNECT

Today I will . . .

- ○ Journal a memory
- ○ Encourage someone
- ○ Walk with someone
- ○ Have a family movie night

CREATE

Today I will . . .

- ○ Build with my hands
- ○ Read something new
- ○ Style a bookshelf
- ○ Create a playlist

MORNING ROUTINE

BEDTIME ROUTINE

PRIORITIES

QUIET REFLECTION

PAUSE · EXAMINE · JOURNAL

WEEK FIVE

HOW WELL DID YOU DO THIS WEEK?

Check the boxes to indicate which rhythms you completed each day. The tallied total will give you a comprehensive view of your week!

	M	T	W	TH	F	S	TOTAL
REST	☐	☐	☐	☐	☐	☐	/6
RESTORE	☐	☐	☐	☐	☐	☐	/6
CONNECT	☐	☐	☐	☐	☐	☐	/6
CREATE	☐	☐	☐	☐	☐	☐	/6

REPLENISH YOUR WEAKEST RHYTHM

Which of the above rhythms did you practice the least and how can you incorporate that rhythm today to be replenished for the week ahead?

WEEKEND REVIEW

REFLECT · ASSESS · LEARN

What did you learn about yourself this week? How were your relationships impacted by your practice of each rhythm?

Which rhythm and activity felt most natural for you? How can this become a part of your routine going forward?

How well did you practice your morning and bedtime routines? What adjustments can you make to ensure you practice these daily?

Check your monthly calendar for upcoming activities and goals.

WEEKEND JOURNAL

DATE

Humble yourselves, then, under God's mighty hand, so that he will lift you up in his own good time. Leave all your worries with him, because he cares for you.

—1 PETER 5:6–7 GNT

MONDAY

DATE

If you are going to be used by God, He will take you through a multitude of experiences that are not meant for you at all, they are meant to make you useful in His hands.

—OSWALD CHAMBERS

REST

Today I will . . .

- ○ Meditate on Scripture
- ○ Reflect and journal
- ○ Read a book
- ○ Stretch my muscles

RESTORE

Today I will . . .

- ○ Stock a fruit bowl
- ○ Take a walk
- ○ Drink 4 glasses of water
- ○ Break a sweat

CONNECT

Today I will . . .

- ○ Write a friend a note
- ○ Encourage someone
- ○ Apologize and forgive
- ○ Pray with someone

CREATE

Today I will . . .

- ○ Journal my goals
- ○ Read something new
- ○ Organize a space
- ○ Daydream

MORNING ROUTINE

BEDTIME ROUTINE

PRIORITIES

QUIET REFLECTION

PAUSE · EXAMINE · JOURNAL

TUESDAY

DATE

We know what we are, but know not what we may be.

—WILLIAM SHAKESPEARE

REST

Today I will . . .

- Enjoy tea or coffee
- Reflect and journal
- Get sunlight
- List today's triumphs

RESTORE

Today I will . . .

- Play an inspiring song
- Take a walk
- Make a salad
- Have a dance party

CONNECT

Today I will . . .

- Work out with a friend
- Encourage someone
- FaceTime a friend
- Make someone laugh

CREATE

Today I will . . .

- Take a class
- Read something new
- Color with a child
- Write down ideas

MORNING ROUTINE

BEDTIME ROUTINE

PRIORITIES

QUIET REFLECTION

PAUSE · EXAMINE · JOURNAL

WEDNESDAY

DATE

The Lord will fulfill his purpose for me.

—PSALM 138:8 ESV

REST

Today I will . . .

- ○ Spend time alone
- ○ Reflect and journal
- ○ Declutter my desk
- ○ Get 8 hours of sleep

RESTORE

Today I will . . .

- ○ Stretch
- ○ Take a walk
- ○ Cook a favorite meal
- ○ Laugh

CONNECT

Today I will . . .

- ○ Give a compliment
- ○ Encourage someone
- ○ Listen intently
- ○ Have coffee with a friend

CREATE

Today I will . . .

- ○ Use my imagination
- ○ Read something new
- ○ Doodle or draw
- ○ Bake something

MORNING ROUTINE

BEDTIME ROUTINE

PRIORITIES

QUIET REFLECTION

PAUSE · EXAMINE · JOURNAL

THURSDAY

DATE

You are worthy to receive something beautiful and you don't have to share it.

—REBEKAH LYONS

REST

Today I will . . .

- ○ Practice contemplative prayer
- ○ Reflect and journal
- ○ Play calming music
- ○ No tech before bed

RESTORE

Today I will . . .

- ○ Cut sugar for the day
- ○ Take a walk
- ○ Do a word search
- ○ Watch a comedy

CONNECT

Today I will . . .

- ○ Enjoy deep conversation
- ○ Encourage someone
- ○ Smile at a stranger
- ○ Dance with someone

CREATE

Today I will . . .

- ○ Write down my dreams
- ○ Read something new
- ○ Play pretend with a child
- ○ Look for inspiration

MORNING ROUTINE

BEDTIME ROUTINE

PRIORITIES

QUIET REFLECTION

PAUSE · EXAMINE · JOURNAL

FRIDAY

DATE

Expect the end of the world. Laugh. Laughter is immeasurable. Be joyful though you have considered all the facts.

—WENDELL BERRY

REST

Today I will . . .

- ○ Confess my fears
- ○ Reflect and journal
- ○ No tech morning
- ○ Take 10 long breaths

RESTORE

Today I will . . .

- ○ Skip watching the news
- ○ Take a walk
- ○ Try a new experience
- ○ Grab an afternoon snack

CONNECT

Today I will . . .

- ○ Have lunch with a friend
- ○ Encourage someone
- ○ Read to a child
- ○ No phones at the table

CREATE

Today I will . . .

- ○ Take photographs
- ○ Read something new
- ○ Make a favorite drink
- ○ Learn something new

MORNING ROUTINE

BEDTIME ROUTINE

PRIORITIES

QUIET REFLECTION

PAUSE · EXAMINE · JOURNAL

SATURDAY

DATE

Memories aren't made from to-do lists.

—AEDRIEL MOXLEY

REST

Today I will . . .

- ○ Light a candle
- ○ Reflect and journal
- ○ Take a nap
- ○ Watch the sunset

RESTORE

Today I will . . .

- ○ Create a meal plan
- ○ Take a walk
- ○ Try a new recipe
- ○ Play a board game

CONNECT

Today I will . . .

- ○ Journal a memory
- ○ Encourage someone
- ○ Walk with someone
- ○ Have a family movie night

CREATE

Today I will . . .

- ○ Build with my hands
- ○ Read something new
- ○ Style a bookshelf
- ○ Create a playlist

MORNING ROUTINE

BEDTIME ROUTINE

PRIORITIES

QUIET REFLECTION

PAUSE · EXAMINE · JOURNAL

WEEK SIX

HOW WELL DID YOU DO THIS WEEK?

Check the boxes to indicate which rhythms you completed each day. The tallied total will give you a comprehensive view of your week!

	M	T	W	TH	F	S	TOTAL
REST	☐	☐	☐	☐	☐	☐	/6
RESTORE	☐	☐	☐	☐	☐	☐	/6
CONNECT	☐	☐	☐	☐	☐	☐	/6
CREATE	☐	☐	☐	☐	☐	☐	/6

REPLENISH YOUR WEAKEST RHYTHM

Which of the above rhythms did you practice the least and how can you incorporate that rhythm today to be replenished for the week ahead?

WEEKEND REVIEW

REFLECT · ASSESS · LEARN

What did you learn about yourself this week? How were your relationships impacted by your practice of each rhythm?

Which rhythm and activity felt most natural for you? How can this become a part of your routine going forward?

How well did you practice your morning and bedtime routines? What adjustments can you make to ensure you practice these daily?

Check your monthly calendar for upcoming activities and goals.

WEEKEND JOURNAL

DATE

Be strong and courageous. Do not be afraid or terrified because of them, for the Lord your God goes with you; he will never leave you nor forsake you.

—DEUTERONOMY 31:6

MONDAY

DATE

In dreams begin responsibilities.

—W. B. YEATS

REST

Today I will . . .

- ○ Meditate on Scripture
- ○ Reflect and journal
- ○ Read a book
- ○ Stretch my muscles

RESTORE

Today I will . . .

- ○ Stock a fruit bowl
- ○ Take a walk
- ○ Drink 4 glasses of water
- ○ Break a sweat

CONNECT

Today I will . . .

- ○ Write a friend a note
- ○ Encourage someone
- ○ Apologize and forgive
- ○ Pray with someone

CREATE

Today I will . . .

- ○ Journal my goals
- ○ Read something new
- ○ Organize a space
- ○ Daydream

MORNING ROUTINE

BEDTIME ROUTINE

PRIORITIES

QUIET REFLECTION

PAUSE · EXAMINE · JOURNAL

TUESDAY

DATE

The place God calls you to is the place where your deep gladness and the world's deep hunger meet.

—FREDERICK BUECHNER

REST

Today I will . . .

- ○ Enjoy tea or coffee
- ○ Reflect and journal
- ○ Get sunlight
- ○ List today's triumphs

RESTORE

Today I will . . .

- ○ Play an inspiring song
- ○ Take a walk
- ○ Make a salad
- ○ Have a dance party

CONNECT

Today I will . . .

- ○ Work out with a friend
- ○ Encourage someone
- ○ FaceTime a friend
- ○ Make someone laugh

CREATE

Today I will . . .

- ○ Take a class
- ○ Read something new
- ○ Color with a child
- ○ Write down ideas

MORNING ROUTINE

BEDTIME ROUTINE

PRIORITIES

QUIET REFLECTION

PAUSE · EXAMINE · JOURNAL

WEDNESDAY

DATE

The two most important days in your life are the day you are born and the day you find out why.

—MARK TWAIN

REST

Today I will . . .

- ○ Spend time alone
- ○ Reflect and journal
- ○ Declutter my desk
- ○ Get 8 hours of sleep

RESTORE

Today I will . . .

- ○ Stretch
- ○ Take a walk
- ○ Cook a favorite meal
- ○ Laugh

CONNECT

Today I will . . .

- ○ Give a compliment
- ○ Encourage someone
- ○ Listen intently
- ○ Have coffee with a friend

CREATE

Today I will . . .

- ○ Use my imagination
- ○ Read something new
- ○ Doodle or draw
- ○ Bake something

MORNING ROUTINE

BEDTIME ROUTINE

PRIORITIES

QUIET REFLECTION

PAUSE · EXAMINE · JOURNAL

THURSDAY

DATE

If the future road looms ominous or unpromising, and the roads back uninviting, then we need to gather our resolve and, carrying only the necessary baggage, step off that road into another direction.

—MAYA ANGELOU

REST

Today I will . . .

- ○ Practice contemplative prayer
- ○ Reflect and journal
- ○ Play calming music
- ○ No tech before bed

RESTORE

Today I will . . .

- ○ Cut sugar for the day
- ○ Take a walk
- ○ Do a word search
- ○ Watch a comedy

CONNECT

Today I will . . .

- ○ Enjoy deep conversation
- ○ Encourage someone
- ○ Smile at a stranger
- ○ Dance with someone

CREATE

Today I will . . .

- ○ Write down my dreams
- ○ Read something new
- ○ Play pretend with a child
- ○ Look for inspiration

MORNING ROUTINE

BEDTIME ROUTINE

PRIORITIES

QUIET REFLECTION

PAUSE · EXAMINE · JOURNAL

FRIDAY

DATE

Tell everyone who is discouraged, "Be strong and don't be afraid! God is coming to your rescue . . ."

—ISAIAH 35:4 GNT

REST

Today I will . . .

- ○ Confess my fears
- ○ Reflect and journal
- ○ No tech morning
- ○ Take 10 long breaths

RESTORE

Today I will . . .

- ○ Skip watching the news
- ○ Take a walk
- ○ Try a new experience
- ○ Grab an afternoon snack

CONNECT

Today I will . . .

- ○ Have lunch with a friend
- ○ Encourage someone
- ○ Read to a child
- ○ No phones at the table

CREATE

Today I will . . .

- ○ Take photographs
- ○ Read something new
- ○ Make a favorite drink
- ○ Learn something new

MORNING ROUTINE

BEDTIME ROUTINE

PRIORITIES

QUIET REFLECTION

PAUSE · EXAMINE · JOURNAL

SATURDAY

DATE

Freedom is found in rest. Rest is found in freedom.

—REBEKAH LYONS

REST

Today I will . . .

- ○ Light a candle
- ○ Reflect and journal
- ○ Take a nap
- ○ Watch the sunset

RESTORE

Today I will . . .

- ○ Create a meal plan
- ○ Take a walk
- ○ Try a new recipe
- ○ Play a board game

CONNECT

Today I will . . .

- ○ Journal a memory
- ○ Encourage someone
- ○ Walk with someone
- ○ Have a family movie night

CREATE

Today I will . . .

- ○ Build with my hands
- ○ Read something new
- ○ Style a bookshelf
- ○ Create a playlist

MORNING ROUTINE

BEDTIME ROUTINE

PRIORITIES

QUIET REFLECTION

PAUSE · EXAMINE · JOURNAL

WEEK SEVEN

HOW WELL DID YOU DO THIS WEEK?

Check the boxes to indicate which rhythms you completed each day. The tallied total will give you a comprehensive view of your week!

	M	T	W	TH	F	S	TOTAL
REST	☐	☐	☐	☐	☐	☐	/6
RESTORE	☐	☐	☐	☐	☐	☐	/6
CONNECT	☐	☐	☐	☐	☐	☐	/6
CREATE	☐	☐	☐	☐	☐	☐	/6

REPLENISH YOUR WEAKEST RHYTHM

Which of the above rhythms did you practice the least and how can you incorporate that rhythm today to be replenished for the week ahead?

WEEKEND REVIEW

REFLECT · ASSESS · LEARN

What did you learn about yourself this week? How were your relationships impacted by your practice of each rhythm?

Which rhythm and activity felt most natural for you? How can this become a part of your routine going forward?

How well did you practice your morning and bedtime routines? What adjustments can you make to ensure you practice these daily?

Check your monthly calendar for upcoming activities and goals.

WEEKEND JOURNAL

DATE

Therefore do not worry about tomorrow,
for tomorrow will worry about itself.
Each day has enough trouble of its own.

—MATTHEW 6:34

MONDAY

DATE

The first hour of the morning is the rudder of the day.

—HENRY WARD BEECHER

REST

Today I will . . .

- ○ Meditate on Scripture
- ○ Reflect and journal
- ○ Read a book
- ○ Stretch my muscles

RESTORE

Today I will . . .

- ○ Stock a fruit bowl
- ○ Take a walk
- ○ Drink 4 glasses of water
- ○ Break a sweat

CONNECT

Today I will . . .

- ○ Write a friend a note
- ○ Encourage someone
- ○ Apologize and forgive
- ○ Pray with someone

CREATE

Today I will . . .

- ○ Journal my goals
- ○ Read something new
- ○ Organize a space
- ○ Daydream

MORNING ROUTINE

BEDTIME ROUTINE

PRIORITIES

QUIET REFLECTION

PAUSE · EXAMINE · JOURNAL

TUESDAY

DATE

You who fear him, trust in the Lord—
he is their help and shield.

—PSALM 115:11

REST

Today I will . . .

- ○ Enjoy tea or coffee
- ○ Reflect and journal
- ○ Get sunlight
- ○ List today's triumphs

RESTORE

Today I will . . .

- ○ Play an inspiring song
- ○ Take a walk
- ○ Make a salad
- ○ Have a dance party

CONNECT

Today I will . . .

- ○ Work out with a friend
- ○ Encourage someone
- ○ FaceTime a friend
- ○ Make someone laugh

CREATE

Today I will . . .

- ○ Take a class
- ○ Read something new
- ○ Color with a child
- ○ Write down ideas

MORNING ROUTINE

BEDTIME ROUTINE

PRIORITIES

QUIET REFLECTION

PAUSE · EXAMINE · JOURNAL

WEDNESDAY

DATE

Freedom is never voluntarily given by the oppressor, it must be demanded by the oppressed.

—MARTIN LUTHER KING JR.

REST

Today I will . . .

- ○ Spend time alone
- ○ Reflect and journal
- ○ Declutter my desk
- ○ Get 8 hours of sleep

RESTORE

Today I will . . .

- ○ Stretch
- ○ Take a walk
- ○ Cook a favorite meal
- ○ Laugh

CONNECT

Today I will . . .

- ○ Give a compliment
- ○ Encourage someone
- ○ Listen intently
- ○ Have coffee with a friend

CREATE

Today I will . . .

- ○ Use my imagination
- ○ Read something new
- ○ Doodle or draw
- ○ Bake something

MORNING ROUTINE

BEDTIME ROUTINE

PRIORITIES

QUIET REFLECTION

PAUSE · EXAMINE · JOURNAL

THURSDAY

DATE

Some people think God does not like to be troubled with our constant coming and asking. The way to trouble God is not to come at all.

—D. L. MOODY

REST

Today I will . . .

- ○ Practice contemplative prayer
- ○ Reflect and journal
- ○ Play calming music
- ○ No tech before bed

RESTORE

Today I will . . .

- ○ Cut sugar for the day
- ○ Take a walk
- ○ Do a word search
- ○ Watch a comedy

CONNECT

Today I will . . .

- ○ Enjoy deep conversation
- ○ Encourage someone
- ○ Smile at a stranger
- ○ Dance with someone

CREATE

Today I will . . .

- ○ Write down my dreams
- ○ Read something new
- ○ Play pretend with a child
- ○ Look for inspiration

MORNING ROUTINE

BEDTIME ROUTINE

PRIORITIES

QUIET REFLECTION

PAUSE · EXAMINE · JOURNAL

FRIDAY

DATE

Apologizing for the wrongs we've committed paves the way for forgiveness in our relationships.

—REBEKAH LYONS

REST

Today I will . . .

- ○ Confess my fears
- ○ Reflect and journal
- ○ No tech morning
- ○ Take 10 long breaths

RESTORE

Today I will . . .

- ○ Skip watching the news
- ○ Take a walk
- ○ Try a new experience
- ○ Grab an afternoon snack

CONNECT

Today I will . . .

- ○ Have lunch with a friend
- ○ Encourage someone
- ○ Read to a child
- ○ No phones at the table

CREATE

Today I will . . .

- ○ Take photographs
- ○ Read something new
- ○ Make a favorite drink
- ○ Learn something new

MORNING ROUTINE

BEDTIME ROUTINE

PRIORITIES

QUIET REFLECTION

PAUSE · EXAMINE · JOURNAL

SATURDAY

DATE

The weaker we feel, the harder we lean. The harder we lean, the stronger we grow spiritually, even while our bodies waste away.

—J. I. PACKER

REST

Today I will . . .

- ○ Light a candle
- ○ Reflect and journal
- ○ Take a nap
- ○ Watch the sunset

RESTORE

Today I will . . .

- ○ Create a meal plan
- ○ Take a walk
- ○ Try a new recipe
- ○ Play a board game

CONNECT

Today I will . . .

- ○ Journal a memory
- ○ Encourage someone
- ○ Walk with someone
- ○ Have a family movie night

CREATE

Today I will . . .

- ○ Build with my hands
- ○ Read something new
- ○ Style a bookshelf
- ○ Create a playlist

MORNING ROUTINE

BEDTIME ROUTINE

PRIORITIES

QUIET REFLECTION

PAUSE · EXAMINE · JOURNAL

WEEK EIGHT

HOW WELL DID YOU DO THIS WEEK?

Check the boxes to indicate which rhythms you completed each day. The tallied total will give you a comprehensive view of your week!

	M	T	W	TH	F	S	TOTAL
REST	☐	☐	☐	☐	☐	☐	/6
RESTORE	☐	☐	☐	☐	☐	☐	/6
CONNECT	☐	☐	☐	☐	☐	☐	/6
CREATE	☐	☐	☐	☐	☐	☐	/6

REPLENISH YOUR WEAKEST RHYTHM

Which of the above rhythms did you practice the least and how can you incorporate that rhythm today to be replenished for the week ahead?

WEEKEND REVIEW

REFLECT · ASSESS · LEARN

What did you learn about yourself this week? How were your relationships impacted by your practice of each rhythm?

Which rhythm and activity felt most natural for you? How can this become a part of your routine going forward?

How well did you practice your morning and bedtime routines? What adjustments can you make to ensure you practice these daily?

Check your monthly calendar for upcoming activities and goals.

WEEKEND JOURNAL

DATE

Even though I walk through the valley of the shadow of death, I will fear no evil, for you are with me; your rod and your staff, they comfort me.

—PSALM 23:4 ESV

MONDAY

DATE

She took the leap and built her wings on the way down.

—KOBI YAMADA

REST

Today I will . . .

- ○ Meditate on Scripture
- ○ Reflect and journal
- ○ Read a book
- ○ Stretch my muscles

RESTORE

Today I will . . .

- ○ Stock a fruit bowl
- ○ Take a walk
- ○ Drink 4 glasses of water
- ○ Break a sweat

CONNECT

Today I will . . .

- ○ Write a friend a note
- ○ Encourage someone
- ○ Apologize and forgive
- ○ Pray with someone

CREATE

Today I will . . .

- ○ Journal my goals
- ○ Read something new
- ○ Organize a space
- ○ Daydream

MORNING ROUTINE

BEDTIME ROUTINE

PRIORITIES

QUIET REFLECTION

PAUSE · EXAMINE · JOURNAL

TUESDAY

DATE

The number one thing that is going to determine your performance is sleep.

—BEN CRANE

REST

Today I will . . .

- ○ Enjoy tea or coffee
- ○ Reflect and journal
- ○ Get sunlight
- ○ List today's triumphs

RESTORE

Today I will . . .

- ○ Play an inspiring song
- ○ Take a walk
- ○ Make a salad
- ○ Have a dance party

CONNECT

Today I will . . .

- ○ Work out with a friend
- ○ Encourage someone
- ○ FaceTime a friend
- ○ Make someone laugh

CREATE

Today I will . . .

- ○ Take a class
- ○ Read something new
- ○ Color with a child
- ○ Write down ideas

MORNING ROUTINE

BEDTIME ROUTINE

PRIORITIES

QUIET REFLECTION

PAUSE · EXAMINE · JOURNAL

WEDNESDAY

DATE

In our waiting, God is working.

—REBEKAH LYONS

REST

Today I will . . .

- ○ Spend time alone
- ○ Reflect and journal
- ○ Declutter my desk
- ○ Get 8 hours of sleep

RESTORE

Today I will . . .

- ○ Stretch
- ○ Take a walk
- ○ Cook a favorite meal
- ○ Laugh

CONNECT

Today I will . . .

- ○ Give a compliment
- ○ Encourage someone
- ○ Listen intently
- ○ Have coffee with a friend

CREATE

Today I will . . .

- ○ Use my imagination
- ○ Read something new
- ○ Doodle or draw
- ○ Bake something

MORNING ROUTINE

BEDTIME ROUTINE

PRIORITIES

QUIET REFLECTION

PAUSE · EXAMINE · JOURNAL

THURSDAY

DATE

The thirstier a man is, the more he'll prize a cup of water; the more our sins break and burden us, the more we'll treasure our Healer and Deliverer.

—THOMAS WILCOX

REST

Today I will . . .

- ○ Practice contemplative prayer
- ○ Reflect and journal
- ○ Play calming music
- ○ No tech before bed

RESTORE

Today I will . . .

- ○ Cut sugar for the day
- ○ Take a walk
- ○ Do a word search
- ○ Watch a comedy

CONNECT

Today I will . . .

- ○ Enjoy deep conversation
- ○ Encourage someone
- ○ Smile at a stranger
- ○ Dance with someone

CREATE

Today I will . . .

- ○ Write down my dreams
- ○ Read something new
- ○ Play pretend with a child
- ○ Look for inspiration

MORNING ROUTINE

BEDTIME ROUTINE

PRIORITIES

QUIET REFLECTION

PAUSE · EXAMINE · JOURNAL

FRIDAY

DATE

The Lord is with me; I will not be afraid. What can mere mortals do to me? The Lord is with me; he is my helper.

—PSALM 118:6–7

REST

Today I will . . .

- ○ Confess my fears
- ○ Reflect and journal
- ○ No tech morning
- ○ Take 10 long breaths

RESTORE

Today I will . . .

- ○ Skip watching the news
- ○ Take a walk
- ○ Try a new experience
- ○ Grab an afternoon snack

CONNECT

Today I will . . .

- ○ Have lunch with a friend
- ○ Encourage someone
- ○ Read to a child
- ○ No phones at the table

CREATE

Today I will . . .

- ○ Take photographs
- ○ Read something new
- ○ Make a favorite drink
- ○ Learn something new

MORNING ROUTINE

BEDTIME ROUTINE

PRIORITIES

QUIET REFLECTION

PAUSE · EXAMINE · JOURNAL

SATURDAY

DATE

God grant me the serenity to accept the things I cannot change, courage to change the things I can, and the wisdom to know the difference.

—REINHOLD NIEBUHR

REST

Today I will . . .

- ○ Light a candle
- ○ Reflect and journal
- ○ Take a nap
- ○ Watch the sunset

RESTORE

Today I will . . .

- ○ Create a meal plan
- ○ Take a walk
- ○ Try a new recipe
- ○ Play a board game

CONNECT

Today I will . . .

- ○ Journal a memory
- ○ Encourage someone
- ○ Walk with someone
- ○ Have a family movie night

CREATE

Today I will . . .

- ○ Build with my hands
- ○ Read something new
- ○ Style a bookshelf
- ○ Create a playlist

MORNING ROUTINE

BEDTIME ROUTINE

PRIORITIES

QUIET REFLECTION

PAUSE · EXAMINE · JOURNAL

SUNDAY

WEEK NINE

HOW WELL DID YOU DO THIS WEEK?

Check the boxes to indicate which rhythms you completed each day. The tallied total will give you a comprehensive view of your week!

	M	T	W	TH	F	S	TOTAL
REST	☐	☐	☐	☐	☐	☐	/6
RESTORE	☐	☐	☐	☐	☐	☐	/6
CONNECT	☐	☐	☐	☐	☐	☐	/6
CREATE	☐	☐	☐	☐	☐	☐	/6

REPLENISH YOUR WEAKEST RHYTHM

Which of the above rhythms did you practice the least and how can you incorporate that rhythm today to be replenished for the week ahead?

WEEKEND REVIEW

REFLECT · ASSESS · LEARN

What did you learn about yourself this week? How were your relationships impacted by your practice of each rhythm?

Which rhythm and activity felt most natural for you? How can this become a part of your routine going forward?

How well did you practice your morning and bedtime routines? What adjustments can you make to ensure you practice these daily?

Check your monthly calendar for upcoming activities and goals.

WEEKEND JOURNAL

DATE

But now, this is what the Lord says . . .
Do not fear, for I have redeemed you; I have
summoned you by name; you are mine.

—ISAIAH 43:1

MONDAY

DATE

Security is mostly a superstition . . . Life is either a daring adventure, or nothing.

—HELEN KELLER

REST

Today I will . . .

- ○ Meditate on Scripture
- ○ Reflect and journal
- ○ Read a book
- ○ Stretch my muscles

RESTORE

Today I will . . .

- ○ Stock a fruit bowl
- ○ Take a walk
- ○ Drink 4 glasses of water
- ○ Break a sweat

CONNECT

Today I will . . .

- ○ Write a friend a note
- ○ Encourage someone
- ○ Apologize and forgive
- ○ Pray with someone

CREATE

Today I will . . .

- ○ Journal my goals
- ○ Read something new
- ○ Organize a space
- ○ Daydream

MORNING ROUTINE

BEDTIME ROUTINE

PRIORITIES

QUIET REFLECTION

PAUSE · EXAMINE · JOURNAL

TUESDAY

DATE

Calling is where your talents and burdens collide.

—REBEKAH LYONS

REST

Today I will . . .

- ○ Enjoy tea or coffee
- ○ Reflect and journal
- ○ Get sunlight
- ○ List today's triumphs

RESTORE

Today I will . . .

- ○ Play an inspiring song
- ○ Take a walk
- ○ Make a salad
- ○ Have a dance party

CONNECT

Today I will . . .

- ○ Work out with a friend
- ○ Encourage someone
- ○ FaceTime a friend
- ○ Make someone laugh

CREATE

Today I will . . .

- ○ Take a class
- ○ Read something new
- ○ Color with a child
- ○ Write down ideas

MORNING ROUTINE

BEDTIME ROUTINE

PRIORITIES

QUIET REFLECTION

PAUSE · EXAMINE · JOURNAL

WEDNESDAY

DATE

Bear one another's burdens.

—THE APOSTLE PAUL

REST

Today I will . . .

- ○ Spend time alone
- ○ Reflect and journal
- ○ Declutter my desk
- ○ Get 8 hours of sleep

RESTORE

Today I will . . .

- ○ Stretch
- ○ Take a walk
- ○ Cook a favorite meal
- ○ Laugh

CONNECT

Today I will . . .

- ○ Give a compliment
- ○ Encourage someone
- ○ Listen intently
- ○ Have coffee with a friend

CREATE

Today I will . . .

- ○ Use my imagination
- ○ Read something new
- ○ Doodle or draw
- ○ Bake something

MORNING ROUTINE

BEDTIME ROUTINE

PRIORITIES

QUIET REFLECTION

PAUSE · EXAMINE · JOURNAL

THURSDAY

DATE

When someone who is both kind and self-serving somehow finds that place within where he or she is still capable of courage and goodness, we get to see something true that we long for.

—ANNE LAMOTT

REST

Today I will . . .

- ○ Practice contemplative prayer
- ○ Reflect and journal
- ○ Play calming music
- ○ No tech before bed

RESTORE

Today I will . . .

- ○ Cut sugar for the day
- ○ Take a walk
- ○ Do a word search
- ○ Watch a comedy

CONNECT

Today I will . . .

- ○ Enjoy deep conversation
- ○ Encourage someone
- ○ Smile at a stranger
- ○ Dance with someone

CREATE

Today I will . . .

- ○ Write down my dreams
- ○ Read something new
- ○ Play pretend with a child
- ○ Look for inspiration

MORNING ROUTINE

BEDTIME ROUTINE

PRIORITIES

QUIET REFLECTION

PAUSE · EXAMINE · JOURNAL

FRIDAY

DATE

Immediately he spoke to them and said, "Take courage! It is I. Don't be afraid."

—MARK 6:50

REST

Today I will . . .

- Confess my fears
- Reflect and journal
- No tech morning
- Take 10 long breaths

RESTORE

Today I will . . .

- Skip watching the news
- Take a walk
- Try a new experience
- Grab an afternoon snack

CONNECT

Today I will . . .

- Have lunch with a friend
- Encourage someone
- Read to a child
- No phones at the table

CREATE

Today I will . . .

- Take photographs
- Read something new
- Make a favorite drink
- Learn something new

MORNING ROUTINE

BEDTIME ROUTINE

PRIORITIES

QUIET REFLECTION

PAUSE · EXAMINE · JOURNAL

SATURDAY

DATE

If you want to bring happiness to the whole world, go home and love your family.

—MOTHER TERESA

REST

Today I will . . .

- ○ Light a candle
- ○ Reflect and journal
- ○ Take a nap
- ○ Watch the sunset

RESTORE

Today I will . . .

- ○ Create a meal plan
- ○ Take a walk
- ○ Try a new recipe
- ○ Play a board game

CONNECT

Today I will . . .

- ○ Journal a memory
- ○ Encourage someone
- ○ Walk with someone
- ○ Have a family movie night

CREATE

Today I will . . .

- ○ Build with my hands
- ○ Read something new
- ○ Style a bookshelf
- ○ Create a playlist

MORNING ROUTINE

BEDTIME ROUTINE

PRIORITIES

QUIET REFLECTION

PAUSE · EXAMINE · JOURNAL

WEEK TEN

HOW WELL DID YOU DO THIS WEEK?

Check the boxes to indicate which rhythms you completed each day. The tallied total will give you a comprehensive view of your week!

	M	T	W	TH	F	S	TOTAL
REST	☐	☐	☐	☐	☐	☐	/6
RESTORE	☐	☐	☐	☐	☐	☐	/6
CONNECT	☐	☐	☐	☐	☐	☐	/6
CREATE	☐	☐	☐	☐	☐	☐	/6

REPLENISH YOUR WEAKEST RHYTHM

Which of the above rhythms did you practice the least and how can you incorporate that rhythm today to be replenished for the week ahead?

WEEKEND REVIEW

REFLECT · ASSESS · LEARN

What did you learn about yourself this week? How were your relationships impacted by your practice of each rhythm?

Which rhythm and activity felt most natural for you? How can this become a part of your routine going forward?

How well did you practice your morning and bedtime routines? What adjustments can you make to ensure you practice these daily?

Check your monthly calendar for upcoming activities and goals.

WEEKEND JOURNAL

DATE

The Lord is my light and my salvation—
whom shall I fear? The Lord is the stronghold
of my life—of whom shall I be afraid?

—PSALM 27:1

MONDAY

DATE

Methinks that the moment my legs begin to move, my thoughts begin to flow.

—HENRY DAVID THOREAU

REST

Today I will . . .

- ○ Meditate on Scripture
- ○ Reflect and journal
- ○ Read a book
- ○ Stretch my muscles

RESTORE

Today I will . . .

- ○ Stock a fruit bowl
- ○ Take a walk
- ○ Drink 4 glasses of water
- ○ Break a sweat

CONNECT

Today I will . . .

- ○ Write a friend a note
- ○ Encourage someone
- ○ Apologize and forgive
- ○ Pray with someone

CREATE

Today I will . . .

- ○ Journal my goals
- ○ Read something new
- ○ Organize a space
- ○ Daydream

MORNING ROUTINE

BEDTIME ROUTINE

PRIORITIES

QUIET REFLECTION

PAUSE · EXAMINE · JOURNAL

TUESDAY

DATE

They will have no fear of bad news; their hearts are steadfast, trusting in the LORD.

—PSALM 112:7

REST

Today I will . . .

- ○ Enjoy tea or coffee
- ○ Reflect and journal
- ○ Get sunlight
- ○ List today's triumphs

RESTORE

Today I will . . .

- ○ Play an inspiring song
- ○ Take a walk
- ○ Make a salad
- ○ Have a dance party

CONNECT

Today I will . . .

- ○ Work out with a friend
- ○ Encourage someone
- ○ FaceTime a friend
- ○ Make someone laugh

CREATE

Today I will . . .

- ○ Take a class
- ○ Read something new
- ○ Color with a child
- ○ Write down ideas

MORNING ROUTINE

BEDTIME ROUTINE

PRIORITIES

QUIET REFLECTION

PAUSE · EXAMINE · JOURNAL

WEDNESDAY

DATE

Death frees from the fear of dying.

—PAULO COELHO

REST

Today I will . . .

- ○ Spend time alone
- ○ Reflect and journal
- ○ Declutter my desk
- ○ Get 8 hours of sleep

RESTORE

Today I will . . .

- ○ Stretch
- ○ Take a walk
- ○ Cook a favorite meal
- ○ Laugh

CONNECT

Today I will . . .

- ○ Give a compliment
- ○ Encourage someone
- ○ Listen intently
- ○ Have coffee with a friend

CREATE

Today I will . . .

- ○ Use my imagination
- ○ Read something new
- ○ Doodle or draw
- ○ Bake something

MORNING ROUTINE

BEDTIME ROUTINE

PRIORITIES

QUIET REFLECTION

PAUSE · EXAMINE · JOURNAL

THURSDAY

DATE

Patience is not an absence of action; rather it is timing. It waits on the right time to act, for the right principles, and in the right way.

—FULTON SHEEN

REST

Today I will . . .

- ○ Practice contemplative prayer
- ○ Reflect and journal
- ○ Play calming music
- ○ No tech before bed

RESTORE

Today I will . . .

- ○ Cut sugar for the day
- ○ Take a walk
- ○ Do a word search
- ○ Watch a comedy

CONNECT

Today I will . . .

- ○ Enjoy deep conversation
- ○ Encourage someone
- ○ Smile at a stranger
- ○ Dance with someone

CREATE

Today I will . . .

- ○ Write down my dreams
- ○ Read something new
- ○ Play pretend with a child
- ○ Look for inspiration

MORNING ROUTINE

BEDTIME ROUTINE

PRIORITIES

QUIET REFLECTION

PAUSE · EXAMINE · JOURNAL

FRIDAY

DATE

To discover something truly great, one must set sail and leave the shore of comfort.

—KHANG KIJARRO NGUYEN

REST

Today I will . . .

- ○ Confess my fears
- ○ Reflect and journal
- ○ No tech morning
- ○ Take 10 long breaths

RESTORE

Today I will . . .

- ○ Skip watching the news
- ○ Take a walk
- ○ Try a new experience
- ○ Grab an afternoon snack

CONNECT

Today I will . . .

- ○ Have lunch with a friend
- ○ Encourage someone
- ○ Read to a child
- ○ No phones at the table

CREATE

Today I will . . .

- ○ Take photographs
- ○ Read something new
- ○ Make a favorite drink
- ○ Learn something new

MORNING ROUTINE

BEDTIME ROUTINE

PRIORITIES

QUIET REFLECTION

PAUSE · EXAMINE · JOURNAL

SATURDAY

DATE

Sabbath is a circuit breaker for idolatry.

—ANDY CROUCH

REST

Today I will . . .

- ○ Light a candle
- ○ Reflect and journal
- ○ Take a nap
- ○ Watch the sunset

RESTORE

Today I will . . .

- ○ Create a meal plan
- ○ Take a walk
- ○ Try a new recipe
- ○ Play a board game

CONNECT

Today I will . . .

- ○ Journal a memory
- ○ Encourage someone
- ○ Walk with someone
- ○ Have a family movie night

CREATE

Today I will . . .

- ○ Build with my hands
- ○ Read something new
- ○ Style a bookshelf
- ○ Create a playlist

MORNING ROUTINE

BEDTIME ROUTINE

PRIORITIES

QUIET REFLECTION

PAUSE · EXAMINE · JOURNAL

SUNDAY

WEEK ELEVEN

HOW WELL DID YOU DO THIS WEEK?

Check the boxes to indicate which rhythms you completed each day. The tallied total will give you a comprehensive view of your week!

	M	T	W	TH	F	S	TOTAL
REST	☐	☐	☐	☐	☐	☐	/6
RESTORE	☐	☐	☐	☐	☐	☐	/6
CONNECT	☐	☐	☐	☐	☐	☐	/6
CREATE	☐	☐	☐	☐	☐	☐	/6

REPLENISH YOUR WEAKEST RHYTHM

Which of the above rhythms did you practice the least and how can you incorporate that rhythm today to be replenished for the week ahead?

WEEKEND REVIEW

REFLECT · ASSESS · LEARN

What did you learn about yourself this week? How were your relationships impacted by your practice of each rhythm?

Which rhythm and activity felt most natural for you? How can this become a part of your routine going forward?

How well did you practice your morning and bedtime routines? What adjustments can you make to ensure you practice these daily?

Check your monthly calendar for upcoming activities and goals.

WEEKEND JOURNAL

DATE

Cast your cares on the Lord and he will sustain you; he will never let the righteous be shaken.

—PSALM 55:22

MONDAY

DATE

If you lose your voice, be quiet a while. It'll come back.

—REBEKAH LYONS

REST

Today I will . . .

- ○ Meditate on Scripture
- ○ Reflect and journal
- ○ Read a book
- ○ Stretch my muscles

RESTORE

Today I will . . .

- ○ Stock a fruit bowl
- ○ Take a walk
- ○ Drink 4 glasses of water
- ○ Break a sweat

CONNECT

Today I will . . .

- ○ Write a friend a note
- ○ Encourage someone
- ○ Apologize and forgive
- ○ Pray with someone

CREATE

Today I will . . .

- ○ Journal my goals
- ○ Read something new
- ○ Organize a space
- ○ Daydream

MORNING ROUTINE

BEDTIME ROUTINE

PRIORITIES

QUIET REFLECTION

PAUSE · EXAMINE · JOURNAL

TUESDAY

DATE

God is our refuge and strength, an ever-present help in trouble.

—PSALM 46:1

REST

Today I will . . .

- ○ Enjoy tea or coffee
- ○ Reflect and journal
- ○ Get sunlight
- ○ List today's triumphs

RESTORE

Today I will . . .

- ○ Play an inspiring song
- ○ Take a walk
- ○ Make a salad
- ○ Have a dance party

CONNECT

Today I will . . .

- ○ Work out with a friend
- ○ Encourage someone
- ○ FaceTime a friend
- ○ Make someone laugh

CREATE

Today I will . . .

- ○ Take a class
- ○ Read something new
- ○ Color with a child
- ○ Write down ideas

MORNING ROUTINE

BEDTIME ROUTINE

PRIORITIES

QUIET REFLECTION

PAUSE · EXAMINE · JOURNAL

WEDNESDAY

DATE

Authenticity is a collection of choices that we have to make every day.

—BRENÉ BROWN

REST

Today I will . . .

- ○ Spend time alone
- ○ Reflect and journal
- ○ Declutter my desk
- ○ Get 8 hours of sleep

RESTORE

Today I will . . .

- ○ Stretch
- ○ Take a walk
- ○ Cook a favorite meal
- ○ Laugh

CONNECT

Today I will . . .

- ○ Give a compliment
- ○ Encourage someone
- ○ Listen intently
- ○ Have coffee with a friend

CREATE

Today I will . . .

- ○ Use my imagination
- ○ Read something new
- ○ Doodle or draw
- ○ Bake something

MORNING ROUTINE

BEDTIME ROUTINE

PRIORITIES

QUIET REFLECTION

PAUSE · EXAMINE · JOURNAL

THURSDAY

DATE

Do not be afraid of them; the LORD *your God himself will fight for you.*

—DEUTERONOMY 3:22

REST

Today I will . . .

- ○ Practice contemplative prayer
- ○ Reflect and journal
- ○ Play calming music
- ○ No tech before bed

RESTORE

Today I will . . .

- ○ Cut sugar for the day
- ○ Take a walk
- ○ Do a word search
- ○ Watch a comedy

CONNECT

Today I will . . .

- ○ Enjoy deep conversation
- ○ Encourage someone
- ○ Smile at a stranger
- ○ Dance with someone

CREATE

Today I will . . .

- ○ Write down my dreams
- ○ Read something new
- ○ Play pretend with a child
- ○ Look for inspiration

MORNING ROUTINE

BEDTIME ROUTINE

PRIORITIES

QUIET REFLECTION

PAUSE · EXAMINE · JOURNAL

FRIDAY

DATE

The wise man in the storm prays to God, not for safety from danger, but deliverance from fear.

—RALPH WALDO EMERSON

REST

Today I will . . .

- ○ Confess my fears
- ○ Reflect and journal
- ○ No tech morning
- ○ Take 10 long breaths

RESTORE

Today I will . . .

- ○ Skip watching the news
- ○ Take a walk
- ○ Try a new experience
- ○ Grab an afternoon snack

CONNECT

Today I will . . .

- ○ Have lunch with a friend
- ○ Encourage someone
- ○ Read to a child
- ○ No phones at the table

CREATE

Today I will . . .

- ○ Take photographs
- ○ Read something new
- ○ Make a favorite drink
- ○ Learn something new

MORNING ROUTINE

BEDTIME ROUTINE

PRIORITIES

QUIET REFLECTION

PAUSE · EXAMINE · JOURNAL

SATURDAY

DATE

When we make memories, we cultivate our imaginations and create memories that outlive us.

—REBEKAH LYONS

REST

Today I will . . .

- ○ Light a candle
- ○ Reflect and journal
- ○ Take a nap
- ○ Watch the sunset

RESTORE

Today I will . . .

- ○ Create a meal plan
- ○ Take a walk
- ○ Try a new recipe
- ○ Play a board game

CONNECT

Today I will . . .

- ○ Journal a memory
- ○ Encourage someone
- ○ Walk with someone
- ○ Have a family movie night

CREATE

Today I will . . .

- ○ Build with my hands
- ○ Read something new
- ○ Style a bookshelf
- ○ Create a playlist

MORNING ROUTINE

BEDTIME ROUTINE

PRIORITIES

QUIET REFLECTION

PAUSE · EXAMINE · JOURNAL

WEEK TWELVE

HOW WELL DID YOU DO THIS WEEK?

Check the boxes to indicate which rhythms you completed each day. The tallied total will give you a comprehensive view of your week!

	M	T	W	TH	F	S	TOTAL
REST	☐	☐	☐	☐	☐	☐	/6
RESTORE	☐	☐	☐	☐	☐	☐	/6
CONNECT	☐	☐	☐	☐	☐	☐	/6
CREATE	☐	☐	☐	☐	☐	☐	/6

REPLENISH YOUR WEAKEST RHYTHM

Which of the above rhythms did you practice the least and how can you incorporate that rhythm today to be replenished for the week ahead?

WEEKEND REVIEW

REFLECT · ASSESS · LEARN

What did you learn about yourself this week? How were your relationships impacted by your practice of each rhythm?

Which rhythm and activity felt most natural for you? How can this become a part of your routine going forward?

How well did you practice your morning and bedtime routines? What adjustments can you make to ensure you practice these daily?

Check your monthly calendar for upcoming activities and goals.

WEEKEND JOURNAL

DATE

But even if you suffer for doing what is right, God will reward you for it. So don't worry or be afraid of their threats.

—1 PETER 3:14 NLT

MONDAY

DATE

"Do not fear, for I myself will help you," declares the Lord, your Redeemer, the Holy One of Israel.

—ISAIAH 41:14

REST

Today I will . . .

- ○ Meditate on Scripture
- ○ Reflect and journal
- ○ Read a book
- ○ Stretch my muscles

RESTORE

Today I will . . .

- ○ Stock a fruit bowl
- ○ Take a walk
- ○ Drink 4 glasses of water
- ○ Break a sweat

CONNECT

Today I will . . .

- ○ Write a friend a note
- ○ Encourage someone
- ○ Apologize and forgive
- ○ Pray with someone

CREATE

Today I will . . .

- ○ Journal my goals
- ○ Read something new
- ○ Organize a space
- ○ Daydream

MORNING ROUTINE

BEDTIME ROUTINE

PRIORITIES

QUIET REFLECTION

PAUSE · EXAMINE · JOURNAL

TUESDAY

DATE

What we discover in healthy solitude is that we're not alone.

—ANDY CROUCH

REST

Today I will . . .

- ○ Enjoy tea or coffee
- ○ Reflect and journal
- ○ Get sunlight
- ○ List today's triumphs

RESTORE

Today I will . . .

- ○ Play an inspiring song
- ○ Take a walk
- ○ Make a salad
- ○ Have a dance party

CONNECT

Today I will . . .

- ○ Work out with a friend
- ○ Encourage someone
- ○ FaceTime a friend
- ○ Make someone laugh

CREATE

Today I will . . .

- ○ Take a class
- ○ Read something new
- ○ Color with a child
- ○ Write down ideas

MORNING ROUTINE

BEDTIME ROUTINE

PRIORITIES

QUIET REFLECTION

PAUSE · EXAMINE · JOURNAL

WEDNESDAY

DATE

Be like the fox, who makes more tracks than necessary, some in the wrong direction. Practice resurrection.

—WENDELL BERRY

REST

Today I will . . .

- ○ Spend time alone
- ○ Reflect and journal
- ○ Declutter my desk
- ○ Get 8 hours of sleep

RESTORE

Today I will . . .

- ○ Stretch
- ○ Take a walk
- ○ Cook a favorite meal
- ○ Laugh

CONNECT

Today I will . . .

- ○ Give a compliment
- ○ Encourage someone
- ○ Listen intently
- ○ Have coffee with a friend

CREATE

Today I will . . .

- ○ Use my imagination
- ○ Read something new
- ○ Doodle or draw
- ○ Bake something

MORNING ROUTINE

BEDTIME ROUTINE

PRIORITIES

QUIET REFLECTION

PAUSE · EXAMINE · JOURNAL

THURSDAY

DATE

When we honestly ask ourselves which person in our lives means the most to us, we often find that it is those who . . . share our pain and touch our wounds with a warm and tender hand.

—HENRI NOUWEN

REST

Today I will . . .

- ○ Practice contemplative prayer
- ○ Reflect and journal
- ○ Play calming music
- ○ No tech before bed

RESTORE

Today I will . . .

- ○ Cut sugar for the day
- ○ Take a walk
- ○ Do a word search
- ○ Watch a comedy

CONNECT

Today I will . . .

- ○ Enjoy deep conversation
- ○ Encourage someone
- ○ Smile at a stranger
- ○ Dance with someone

CREATE

Today I will . . .

- ○ Write down my dreams
- ○ Read something new
- ○ Play pretend with a child
- ○ Look for inspiration

MORNING ROUTINE

BEDTIME ROUTINE

PRIORITIES

QUIET REFLECTION

PAUSE · EXAMINE · JOURNAL

FRIDAY

DATE

I will no longer act on the outside in a way that contradicts the truth I hold deeply on the inside. I will no longer act as if I were less than the whole person I know myself inwardly to be.

—ROSA PARKS

REST

Today I will . . .

- ○ Confess my fears
- ○ Reflect and journal
- ○ No tech morning
- ○ Take 10 long breaths

RESTORE

Today I will . . .

- ○ Skip watching the news
- ○ Take a walk
- ○ Try a new experience
- ○ Grab an afternoon snack

CONNECT

Today I will . . .

- ○ Have lunch with a friend
- ○ Encourage someone
- ○ Read to a child
- ○ No phones at the table

CREATE

Today I will . . .

- ○ Take photographs
- ○ Read something new
- ○ Make a favorite drink
- ○ Learn something new

MORNING ROUTINE

BEDTIME ROUTINE

PRIORITIES

QUIET REFLECTION

PAUSE · EXAMINE · JOURNAL

SATURDAY

DATE

When we give ourselves new experiences, we begin to expand our thinking and creativity.

—REBEKAH LYONS

REST

Today I will . . .

- ○ Light a candle
- ○ Reflect and journal
- ○ Take a nap
- ○ Watch the sunset

RESTORE

Today I will . . .

- ○ Create a meal plan
- ○ Take a walk
- ○ Try a new recipe
- ○ Play a board game

CONNECT

Today I will . . .

- ○ Journal a memory
- ○ Encourage someone
- ○ Walk with someone
- ○ Have a family movie night

CREATE

Today I will . . .

- ○ Build with my hands
- ○ Read something new
- ○ Style a bookshelf
- ○ Create a playlist

MORNING ROUTINE

BEDTIME ROUTINE

PRIORITIES

QUIET REFLECTION

PAUSE · EXAMINE · JOURNAL

SUNDAY

WEEK THIRTEEN

HOW WELL DID YOU DO THIS WEEK?

Check the boxes to indicate which rhythms you completed each day. The tallied total will give you a comprehensive view of your week!

	M	T	W	TH	F	S	TOTAL
REST	☐	☐	☐	☐	☐	☐	/6
RESTORE	☐	☐	☐	☐	☐	☐	/6
CONNECT	☐	☐	☐	☐	☐	☐	/6
CREATE	☐	☐	☐	☐	☐	☐	/6

REPLENISH YOUR WEAKEST RHYTHM

Which of the above rhythms did you practice the least and how can you incorporate that rhythm today to be replenished for the week ahead?

WEEKEND REVIEW

REFLECT · ASSESS · LEARN

What did you learn about yourself this week? How were your relationships impacted by your practice of each rhythm?

Which rhythm and activity felt most natural for you? How can this become a part of your routine going forward?

How well did you practice your morning and bedtime routines? What adjustments can you make to ensure you practice these daily?

Check your monthly calendar for upcoming activities and goals.

WEEKEND JOURNAL

DATE

Do not be afraid. I am the
First and the Last.

—REVELATION 1:17

MONDAY

DATE

We were designed to dream, and to take responsibility for those dreams.

—REBEKAH LYONS

REST

Today I will . . .

- ○ Meditate on Scripture
- ○ Reflect and journal
- ○ Read a book
- ○ Stretch my muscles

RESTORE

Today I will . . .

- ○ Stock a fruit bowl
- ○ Take a walk
- ○ Drink 4 glasses of water
- ○ Break a sweat

CONNECT

Today I will . . .

- ○ Write a friend a note
- ○ Encourage someone
- ○ Apologize and forgive
- ○ Pray with someone

CREATE

Today I will . . .

- ○ Journal my goals
- ○ Read something new
- ○ Organize a space
- ○ Daydream

MORNING ROUTINE

BEDTIME ROUTINE

PRIORITIES

QUIET REFLECTION

PAUSE · EXAMINE · JOURNAL

TUESDAY

DATE

Anyone who stops learning is old, whether at twenty or eighty.

—HENRY FORD

REST

Today I will . . .

- ○ Enjoy tea or coffee
- ○ Reflect and journal
- ○ Get sunlight
- ○ List today's triumphs

RESTORE

Today I will . . .

- ○ Play an inspiring song
- ○ Take a walk
- ○ Make a salad
- ○ Have a dance party

CONNECT

Today I will . . .

- ○ Work out with a friend
- ○ Encourage someone
- ○ FaceTime a friend
- ○ Make someone laugh

CREATE

Today I will . . .

- ○ Take a class
- ○ Read something new
- ○ Color with a child
- ○ Write down ideas

MORNING ROUTINE

BEDTIME ROUTINE

PRIORITIES

QUIET REFLECTION

PAUSE · EXAMINE · JOURNAL

WEDNESDAY

DATE

We become what we pay attention to.

—CURT THOMPSON, MD

REST

Today I will . . .

- ○ Spend time alone
- ○ Reflect and journal
- ○ Declutter my desk
- ○ Get 8 hours of sleep

RESTORE

Today I will . . .

- ○ Stretch
- ○ Take a walk
- ○ Cook a favorite meal
- ○ Laugh

CONNECT

Today I will . . .

- ○ Give a compliment
- ○ Encourage someone
- ○ Listen intently
- ○ Have coffee with a friend

CREATE

Today I will . . .

- ○ Use my imagination
- ○ Read something new
- ○ Doodle or draw
- ○ Bake something

MORNING ROUTINE

BEDTIME ROUTINE

PRIORITIES

QUIET REFLECTION

PAUSE · EXAMINE · JOURNAL

THURSDAY

DATE

It is not trying that is ever going to bring us home. All this trying leads up to the vital moment at which you turn to God and say, "You must do this. I can't."

—C. S. LEWIS

REST

Today I will . . .

- ○ Practice contemplative prayer
- ○ Reflect and journal
- ○ Play calming music
- ○ No tech before bed

RESTORE

Today I will . . .

- ○ Cut sugar for the day
- ○ Take a walk
- ○ Do a word search
- ○ Watch a comedy

CONNECT

Today I will . . .

- ○ Enjoy deep conversation
- ○ Encourage someone
- ○ Smile at a stranger
- ○ Dance with someone

CREATE

Today I will . . .

- ○ Write down my dreams
- ○ Read something new
- ○ Play pretend with a child
- ○ Look for inspiration

MORNING ROUTINE

BEDTIME ROUTINE

PRIORITIES

QUIET REFLECTION

PAUSE · EXAMINE · JOURNAL

FRIDAY

DATE

The angel of the Lord encamps around those who fear him, and he delivers them.

—PSALM 34:7

REST

Today I will . . .

- ○ Confess my fears
- ○ Reflect and journal
- ○ No tech morning
- ○ Take 10 long breaths

RESTORE

Today I will . . .

- ○ Skip watching the news
- ○ Take a walk
- ○ Try a new experience
- ○ Grab an afternoon snack

CONNECT

Today I will . . .

- ○ Have lunch with a friend
- ○ Encourage someone
- ○ Read to a child
- ○ No phones at the table

CREATE

Today I will . . .

- ○ Take photographs
- ○ Read something new
- ○ Make a favorite drink
- ○ Learn something new

MORNING ROUTINE

BEDTIME ROUTINE

PRIORITIES

QUIET REFLECTION

PAUSE · EXAMINE · JOURNAL

SATURDAY

DATE

Most things we create take community and connection.

—GABE LYONS

REST

Today I will . . .

- ○ Light a candle
- ○ Reflect and journal
- ○ Take a nap
- ○ Watch the sunset

RESTORE

Today I will . . .

- ○ Create a meal plan
- ○ Take a walk
- ○ Try a new recipe
- ○ Play a board game

CONNECT

Today I will . . .

- ○ Journal a memory
- ○ Encourage someone
- ○ Walk with someone
- ○ Have a family movie night

CREATE

Today I will . . .

- ○ Build with my hands
- ○ Read something new
- ○ Style a bookshelf
- ○ Create a playlist

MORNING ROUTINE

BEDTIME ROUTINE

PRIORITIES

QUIET REFLECTION

PAUSE · EXAMINE · JOURNAL

SUNDAY

WEEK FOURTEEN

HOW WELL DID YOU DO THIS WEEK?

Check the boxes to indicate which rhythms you completed each day. The tallied total will give you a comprehensive view of your week!

	M	T	W	TH	F	S	TOTAL
REST	☐	☐	☐	☐	☐	☐	/6
RESTORE	☐	☐	☐	☐	☐	☐	/6
CONNECT	☐	☐	☐	☐	☐	☐	/6
CREATE	☐	☐	☐	☐	☐	☐	/6

REPLENISH YOUR WEAKEST RHYTHM

Which of the above rhythms did you practice the least and how can you incorporate that rhythm today to be replenished for the week ahead?

WEEKEND REVIEW

REFLECT · ASSESS · LEARN

What did you learn about yourself this week? How were your relationships impacted by your practice of each rhythm?

Which rhythm and activity felt most natural for you? How can this become a part of your routine going forward?

How well did you practice your morning and bedtime routines? What adjustments can you make to ensure you practice these daily?

Check your monthly calendar for upcoming activities and goals.

WEEKEND JOURNAL

DATE

Jesus told him,
"Don't be afraid; just believe."

—MARK 5:36

MONDAY

DATE

The more that you read, the more things you will know.
The more that you learn, the more places you'll go.

—DR. SEUSS

REST

Today I will . . .

- ○ Meditate on Scripture
- ○ Reflect and journal
- ○ Read a book
- ○ Stretch my muscles

RESTORE

Today I will . . .

- ○ Stock a fruit bowl
- ○ Take a walk
- ○ Drink 4 glasses of water
- ○ Break a sweat

CONNECT

Today I will . . .

- ○ Write a friend a note
- ○ Encourage someone
- ○ Apologize and forgive
- ○ Pray with someone

CREATE

Today I will . . .

- ○ Journal my goals
- ○ Read something new
- ○ Organize a space
- ○ Daydream

MORNING ROUTINE

BEDTIME ROUTINE

PRIORITIES

QUIET REFLECTION

PAUSE · EXAMINE · JOURNAL

TUESDAY

DATE

We're all trying to point to beauty in different ways.

—RYAN O'NEAL

REST

Today I will . . .

- ○ Enjoy tea or coffee
- ○ Reflect and journal
- ○ Get sunlight
- ○ List today's triumphs

RESTORE

Today I will . . .

- ○ Play an inspiring song
- ○ Take a walk
- ○ Make a salad
- ○ Have a dance party

CONNECT

Today I will . . .

- ○ Work out with a friend
- ○ Encourage someone
- ○ FaceTime a friend
- ○ Make someone laugh

CREATE

Today I will . . .

- ○ Take a class
- ○ Read something new
- ○ Color with a child
- ○ Write down ideas

MORNING ROUTINE

BEDTIME ROUTINE

PRIORITIES

QUIET REFLECTION

PAUSE · EXAMINE · JOURNAL

WEDNESDAY

DATE

You cannot heal what is hidden, but when you confess something out loud, you bring it into the light, where it can be healed.

—REBEKAH LYONS

REST

Today I will . . .

- ○ Spend time alone
- ○ Reflect and journal
- ○ Declutter my desk
- ○ Get 8 hours of sleep

RESTORE

Today I will . . .

- ○ Stretch
- ○ Take a walk
- ○ Cook a favorite meal
- ○ Laugh

CONNECT

Today I will . . .

- ○ Give a compliment
- ○ Encourage someone
- ○ Listen intently
- ○ Have coffee with a friend

CREATE

Today I will . . .

- ○ Use my imagination
- ○ Read something new
- ○ Doodle or draw
- ○ Bake something

MORNING ROUTINE

BEDTIME ROUTINE

PRIORITIES

QUIET REFLECTION

PAUSE · EXAMINE · JOURNAL

THURSDAY

DATE

I prayed to the Lord, and he answered me.
He freed me from all my fears.

—PSALM 34:4 GNT

REST

Today I will . . .

- ○ Practice contemplative prayer
- ○ Reflect and journal
- ○ Play calming music
- ○ No tech before bed

RESTORE

Today I will . . .

- ○ Cut sugar for the day
- ○ Take a walk
- ○ Do a word search
- ○ Watch a comedy

CONNECT

Today I will . . .

- ○ Enjoy deep conversation
- ○ Encourage someone
- ○ Smile at a stranger
- ○ Dance with someone

CREATE

Today I will . . .

- ○ Write down my dreams
- ○ Read something new
- ○ Play pretend with a child
- ○ Look for inspiration

MORNING ROUTINE

BEDTIME ROUTINE

PRIORITIES

QUIET REFLECTION

PAUSE · EXAMINE · JOURNAL

FRIDAY

DATE

When you can celebrate and don't have to compare, it unlocks the freedom to find joy.

—SADIE ROBERTSON

REST

Today I will . . .

- ○ Confess my fears
- ○ Reflect and journal
- ○ No tech morning
- ○ Take 10 long breaths

RESTORE

Today I will . . .

- ○ Skip watching the news
- ○ Take a walk
- ○ Try a new experience
- ○ Grab an afternoon snack

CONNECT

Today I will . . .

- ○ Have lunch with a friend
- ○ Encourage someone
- ○ Read to a child
- ○ No phones at the table

CREATE

Today I will . . .

- ○ Take photographs
- ○ Read something new
- ○ Make a favorite drink
- ○ Learn something new

MORNING ROUTINE

BEDTIME ROUTINE

PRIORITIES

QUIET REFLECTION

PAUSE · EXAMINE · JOURNAL

SATURDAY

DATE

Asking awakens our holy imagination to God's divine intervention.

—REBEKAH LYONS

REST

Today I will . . .

- ○ Light a candle
- ○ Reflect and journal
- ○ Take a nap
- ○ Watch the sunset

RESTORE

Today I will . . .

- ○ Create a meal plan
- ○ Take a walk
- ○ Try a new recipe
- ○ Play a board game

CONNECT

Today I will . . .

- ○ Journal a memory
- ○ Encourage someone
- ○ Walk with someone
- ○ Have a family movie night

CREATE

Today I will . . .

- ○ Build with my hands
- ○ Read something new
- ○ Style a bookshelf
- ○ Create a playlist

MORNING ROUTINE

BEDTIME ROUTINE

PRIORITIES

QUIET REFLECTION

PAUSE · EXAMINE · JOURNAL

SUNDAY

WEEK FIFTEEN

HOW WELL DID YOU DO THIS WEEK?

Check the boxes to indicate which rhythms you completed each day. The tallied total will give you a comprehensive view of your week!

	M	T	W	TH	F	S	TOTAL
REST	☐	☐	☐	☐	☐	☐	/6
RESTORE	☐	☐	☐	☐	☐	☐	/6
CONNECT	☐	☐	☐	☐	☐	☐	/6
CREATE	☐	☐	☐	☐	☐	☐	/6

REPLENISH YOUR WEAKEST RHYTHM

Which of the above rhythms did you practice the least and how can you incorporate that rhythm today to be replenished for the week ahead?

WEEKEND REVIEW

REFLECT · ASSESS · LEARN

What did you learn about yourself this week? How were your relationships impacted by your practice of each rhythm?

Which rhythm and activity felt most natural for you? How can this become a part of your routine going forward?

How well did you practice your morning and bedtime routines? What adjustments can you make to ensure you practice these daily?

Check your monthly calendar for upcoming activities and goals.

WEEKEND JOURNAL

DATE

Peace is what I leave with you;
it is my own peace that I give you.
I do not give it as the world does.

—JOHN 14:27 GNT

QUARTERLY REFLECTION

Well done! You've taken three months to commit to prioritizing your mental health. Are you feeling more rested, restored, connected, and creative? Less anxious, worried, and stressed?

Take time to listen, reflect, and assess. Identify and describe how well you did implementing the Rhythm system this past quarter, as well as how you plan to improve next quarter.

REST

I experienced this rhythm best when:

I want to improve next quarter by:

RESTORE

I experienced this rhythm best when:

I want to improve next quarter by:

QUARTERLY RHYTHM RATING

On a scale of 1 to 10, circle how effective you were with each rhythm:

REST	1	2	3	4	5	6	7	8	9	10
RESTORE	1	2	3	4	5	6	7	8	9	10
CONNECT	1	2	3	4	5	6	7	8	9	10
CREATE	1	2	3	4	5	6	7	8	9	10

CONNECT

I experienced this rhythm best when:

I want to improve next quarter by:

CREATE

I experienced this rhythm best when:

I want to improve next quarter by:

CONGRATULATIONS!

You've completed the Rhythm system for this quarter.

To order your *Rhythms for Life Planner & Journal* for a new quarter, visit:

WWW.REBEKAHLYONS.COM